AF572034

Paint Box

A Colorful Romance

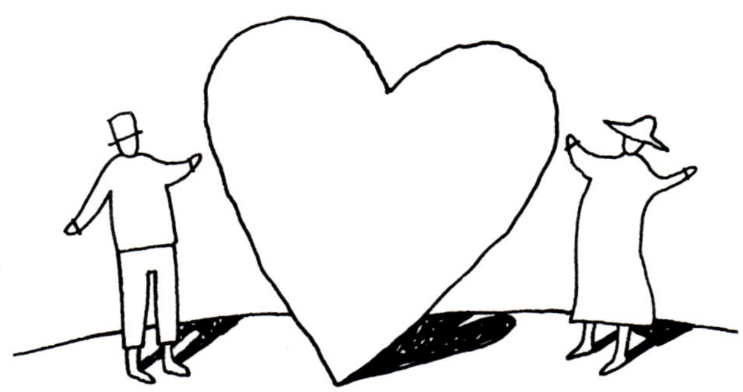

Debbie Tomassi

Paint Box

A Colorful Romance

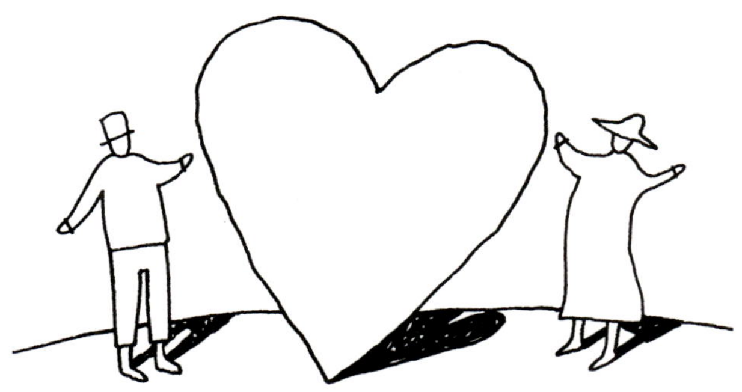

Debbie Tomassi

A BULFINCH PRESS BOOK
Little, Brown and Company
Boston New York London

First edition

Library of Congress Cataloging-in-Publication Data
Tomassi, Debbie.
Paint box : a colorful romance / by Debbie Tomassi. — 1st ed.
p. cm.
ISBN 0-8212-2482-4 (hardcover)
1. Tomassi, Debbie — Themes, motives. 2. Love in art. I. Title.
ND1839. T65A4 1998
759.13 — dc21 98-13419

Type design by Barbara Koster

Bulfinch Press is an imprint and trademark of Little, Brown and Company (Inc.)

PRINTED IN HONG KONG

For Tony

Her Paint Box

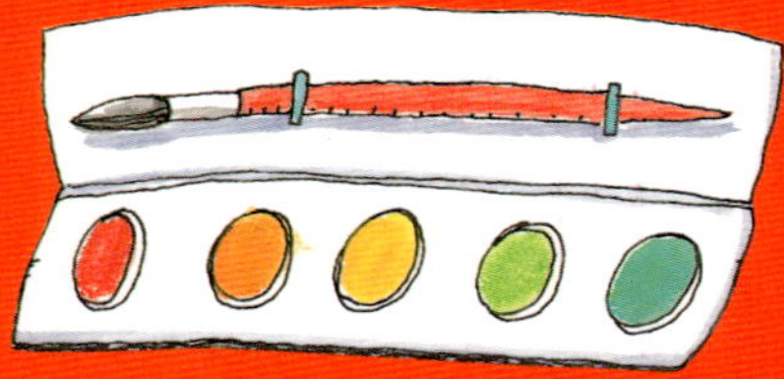

Her paint box was full of many colors, the brightest of hues.

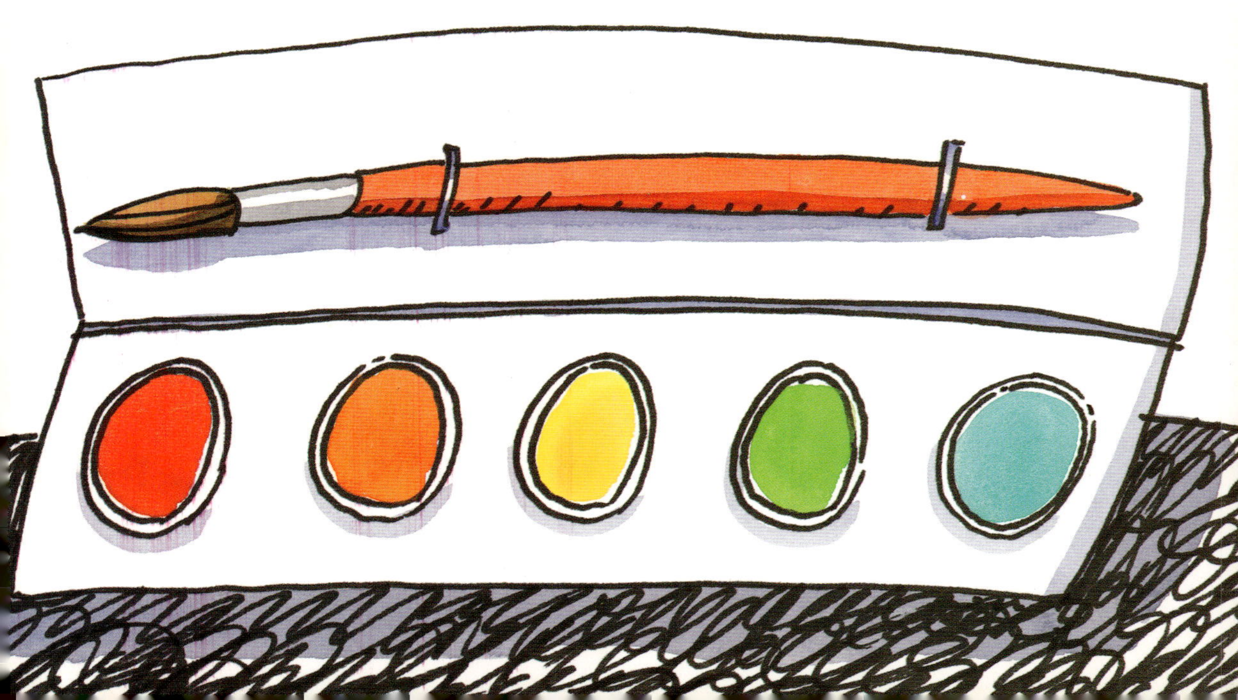

She brought the box with her everywhere she went

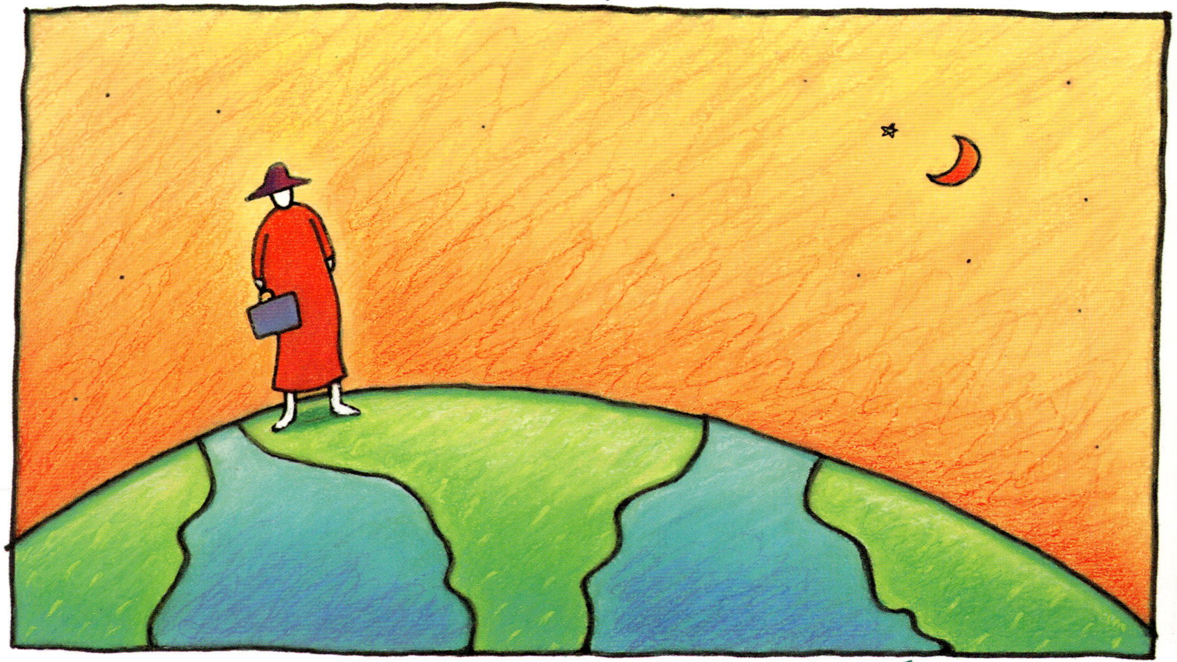

and used it to color her world.

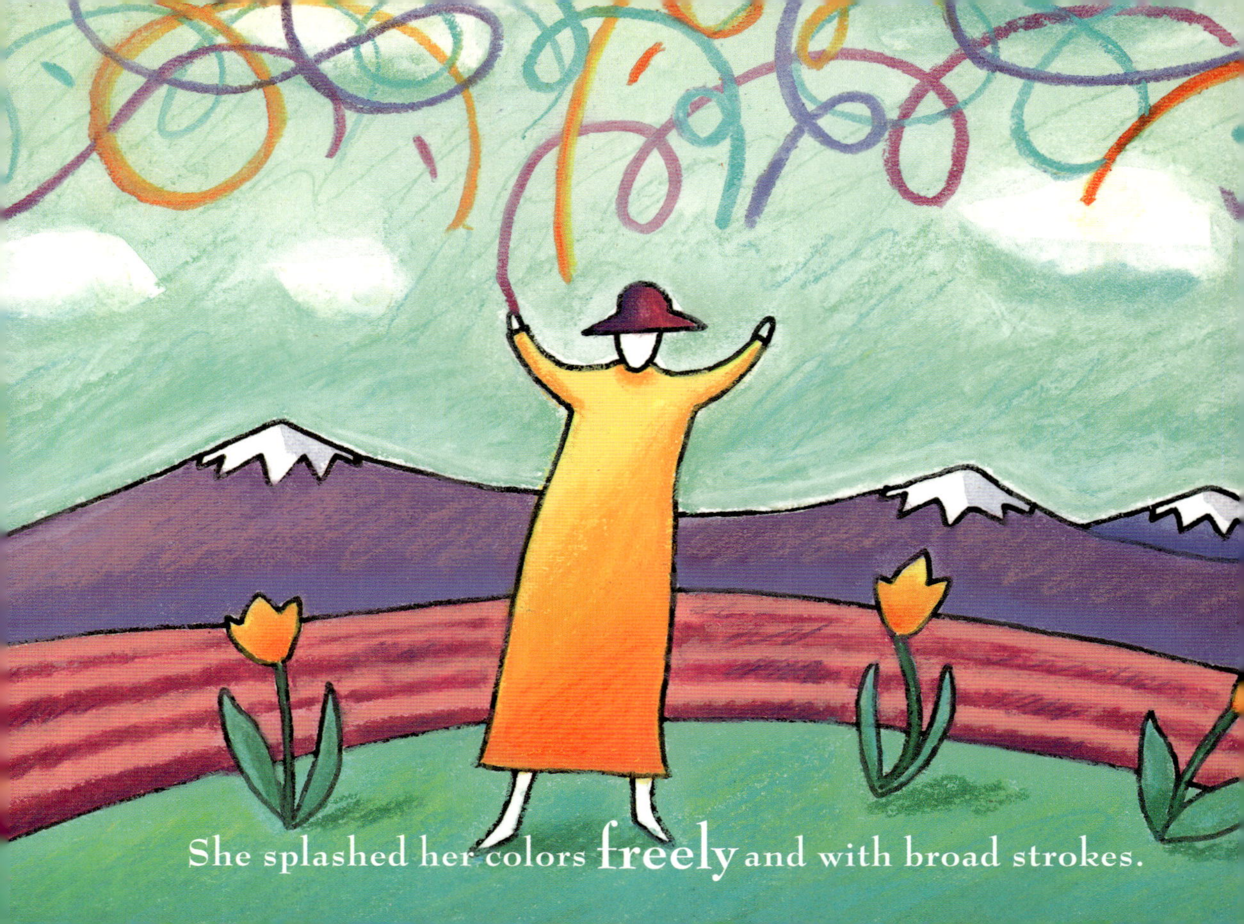

She splashed her colors **freely** and with broad strokes.

She painted the sky with rainbows.

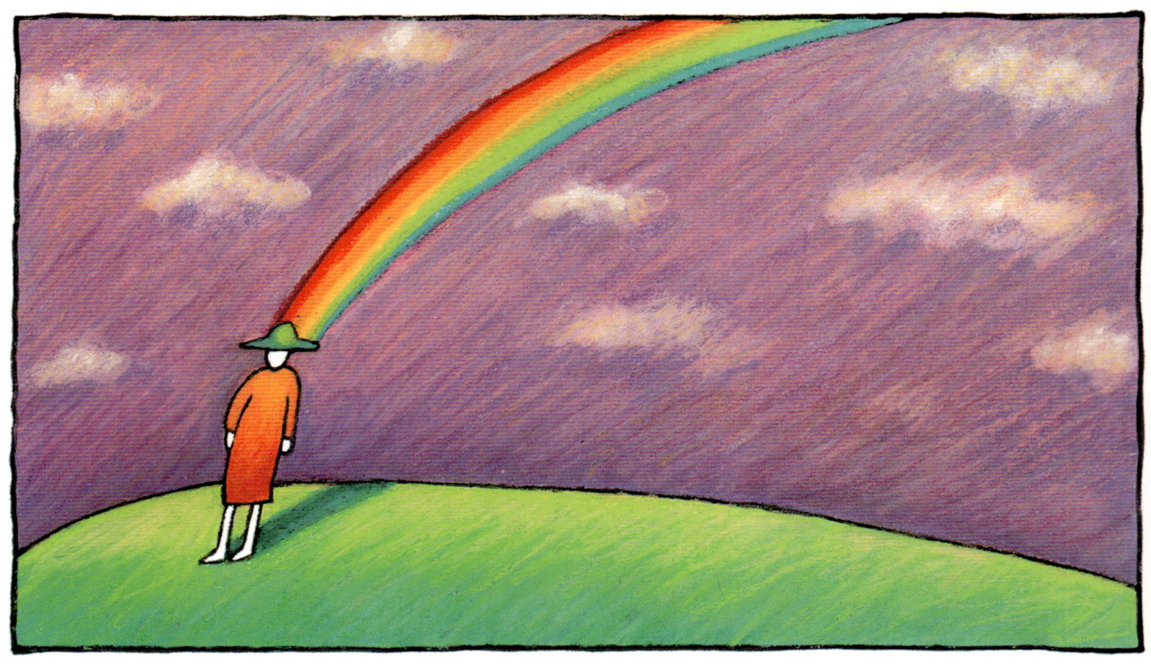

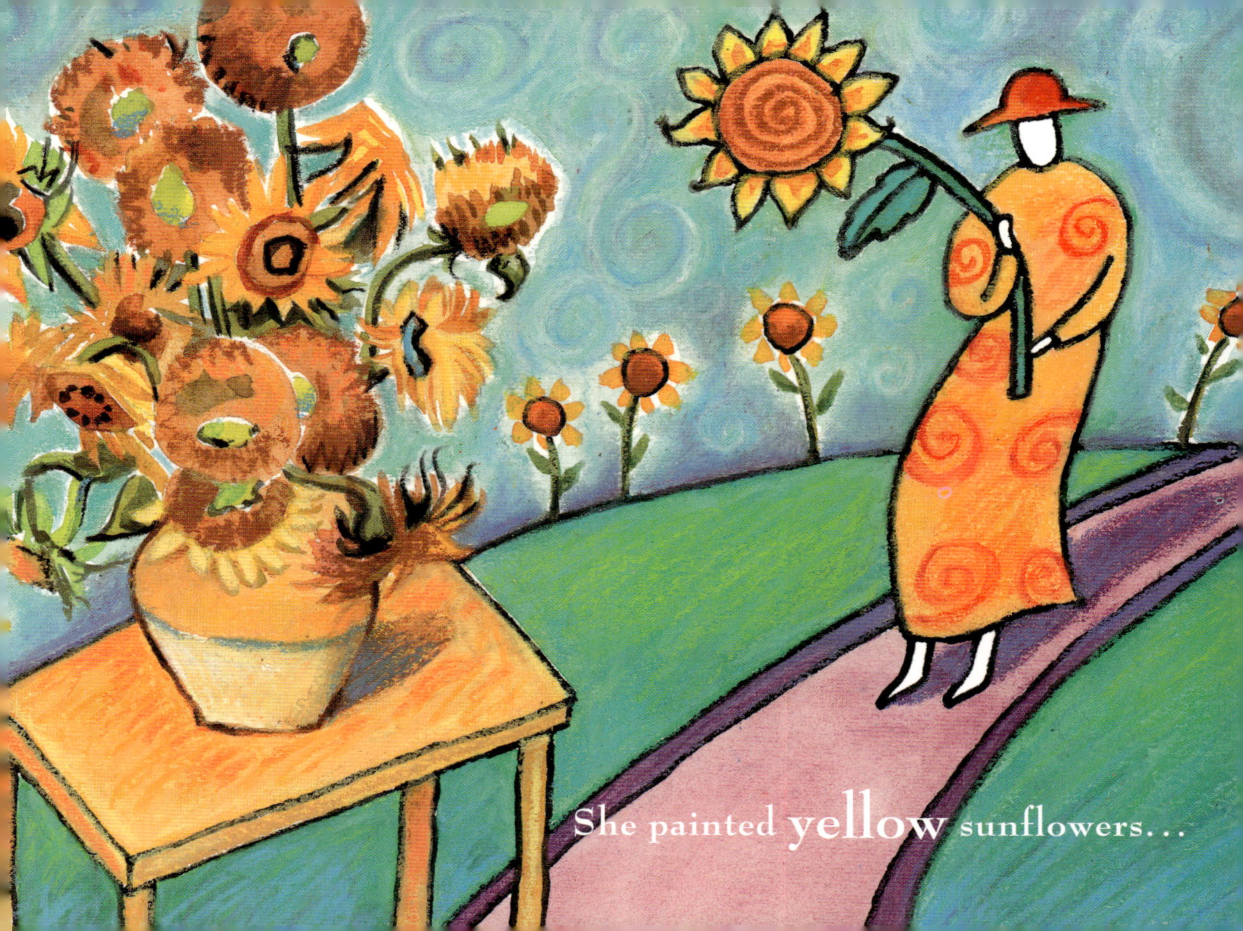

She painted **yellow** sunflowers…

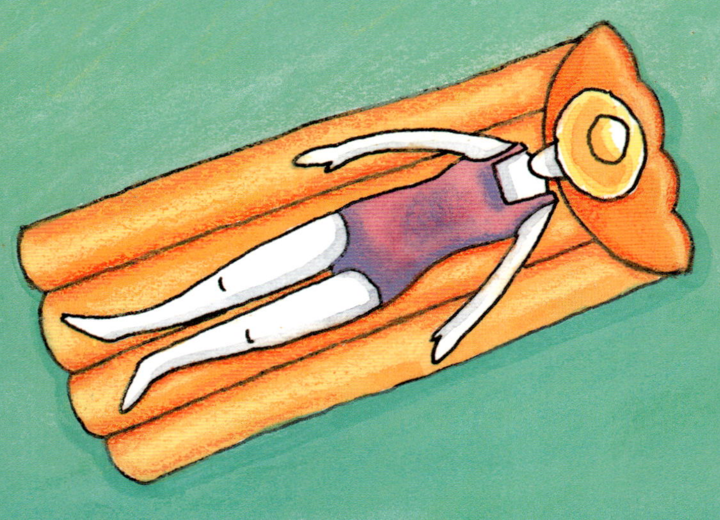

and vivid **blue** oceans.

She surrounded herself in passionate

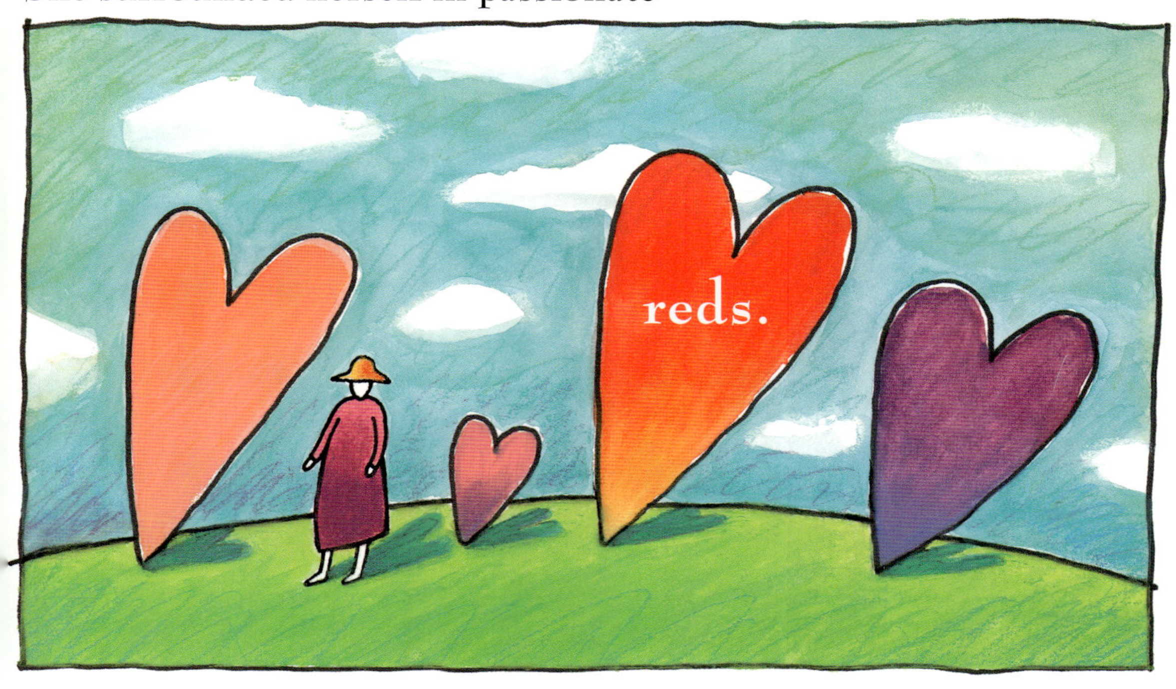

reds.

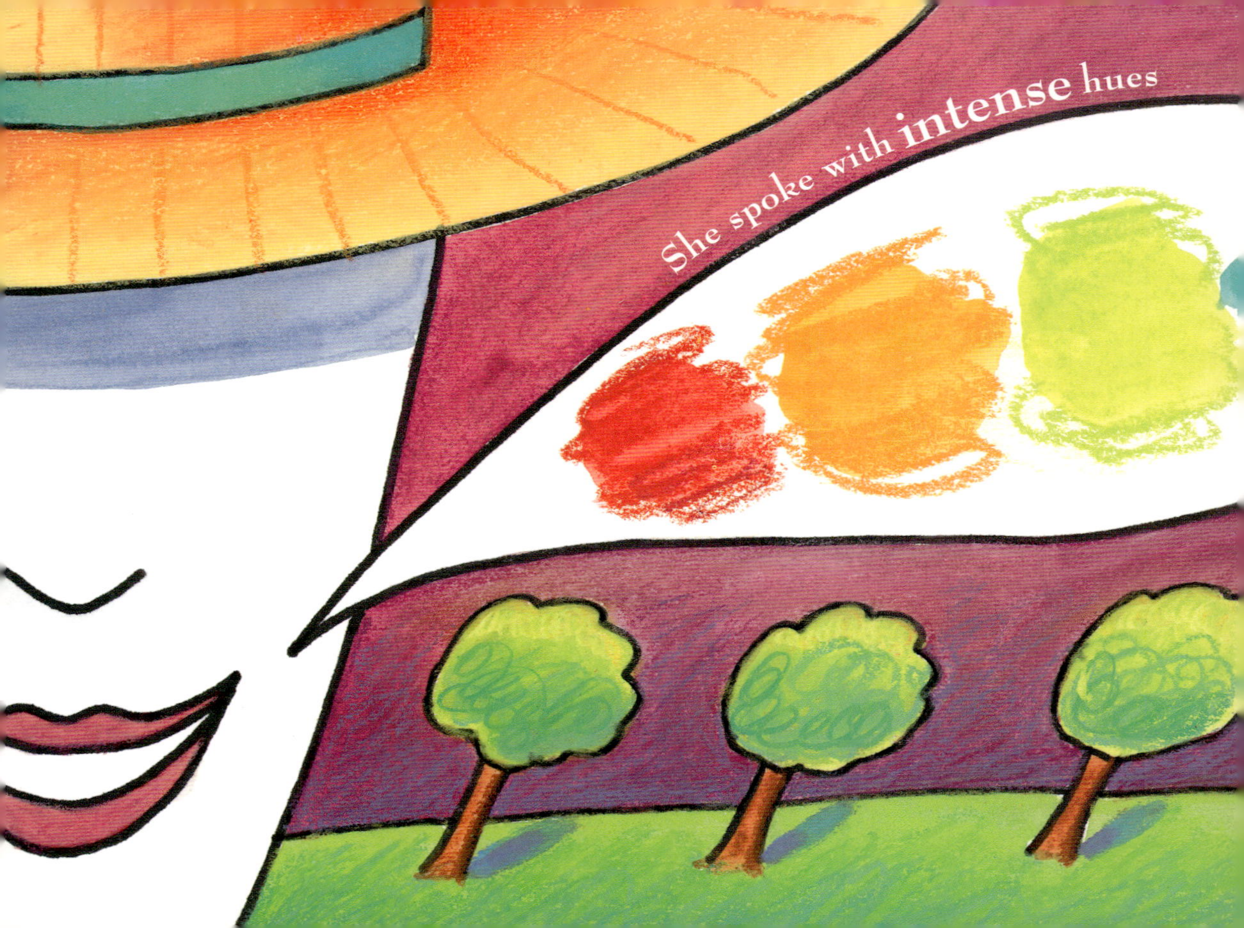
She spoke with intense hues

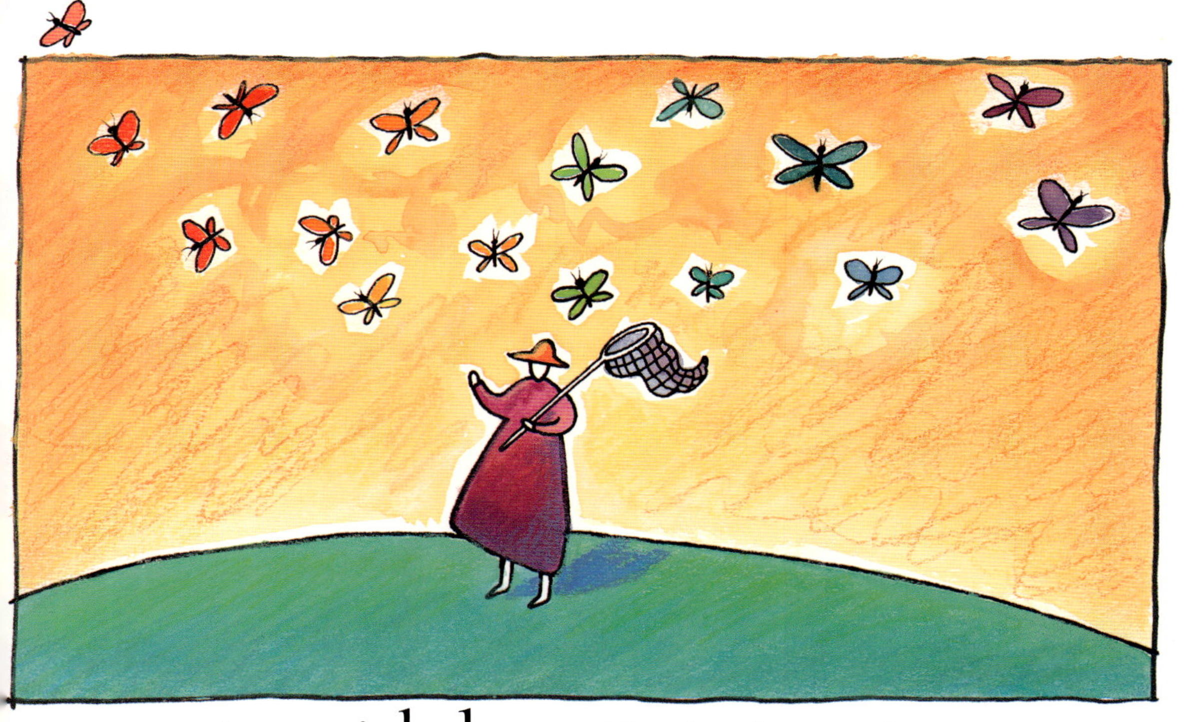

that **swirled** around her head in a vibrant spectrum.

Her paints **tumbled** through the air like bright autumn leaves

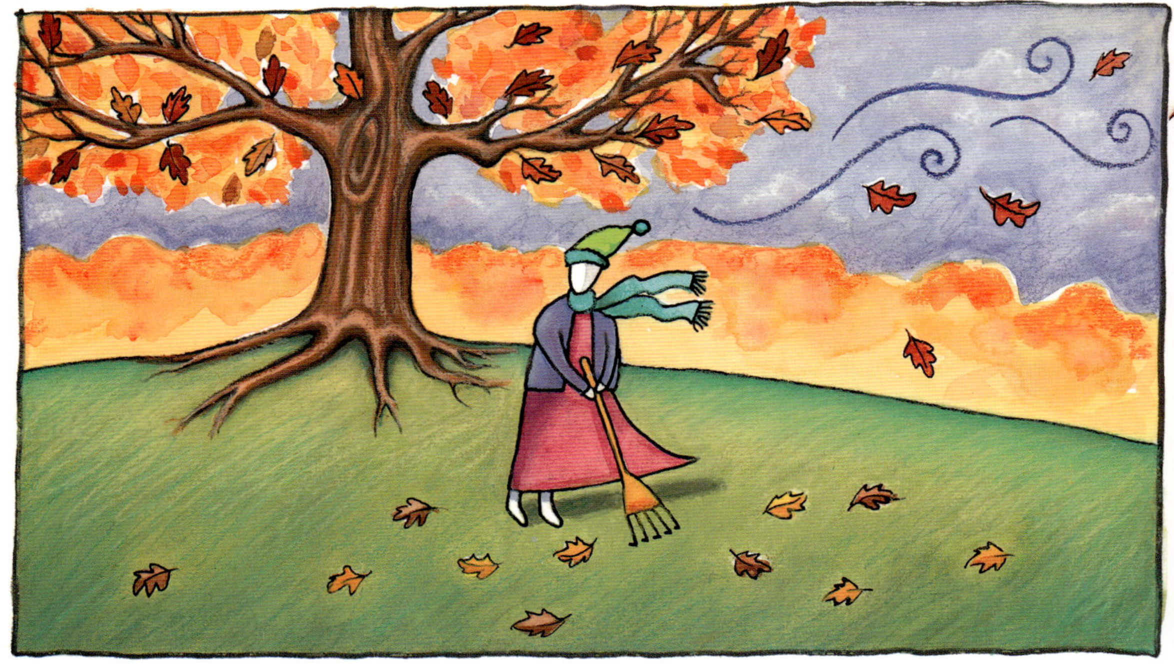

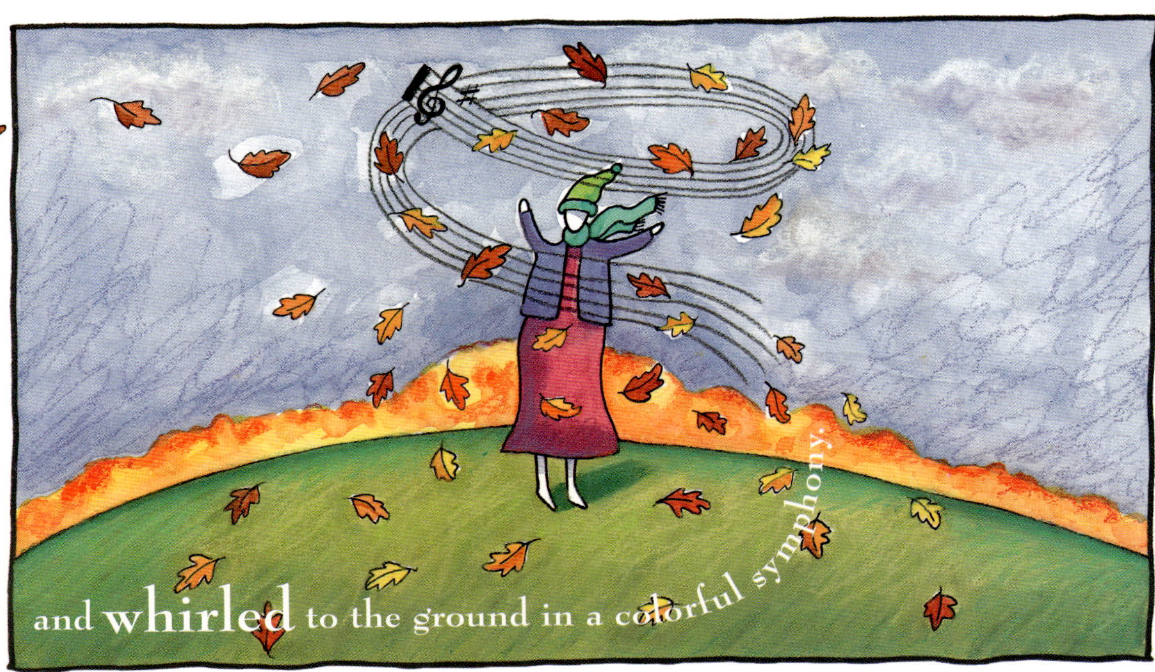

and **whirled** to the ground in a colorful symphony.

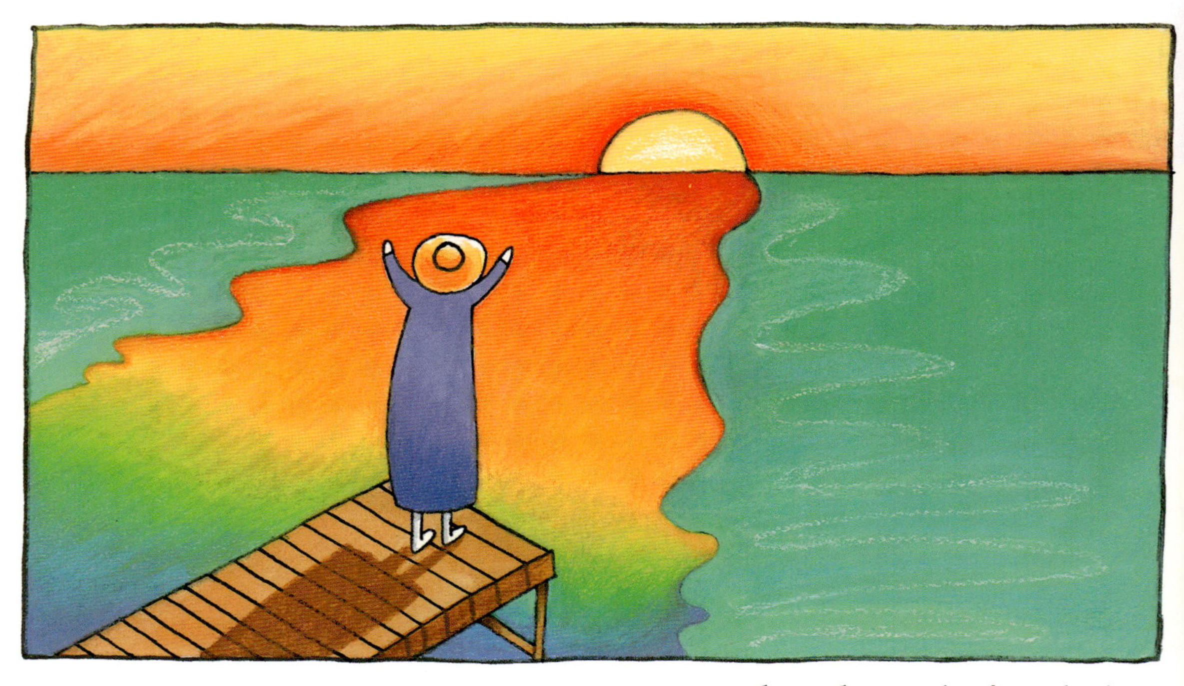

And at the end of each day

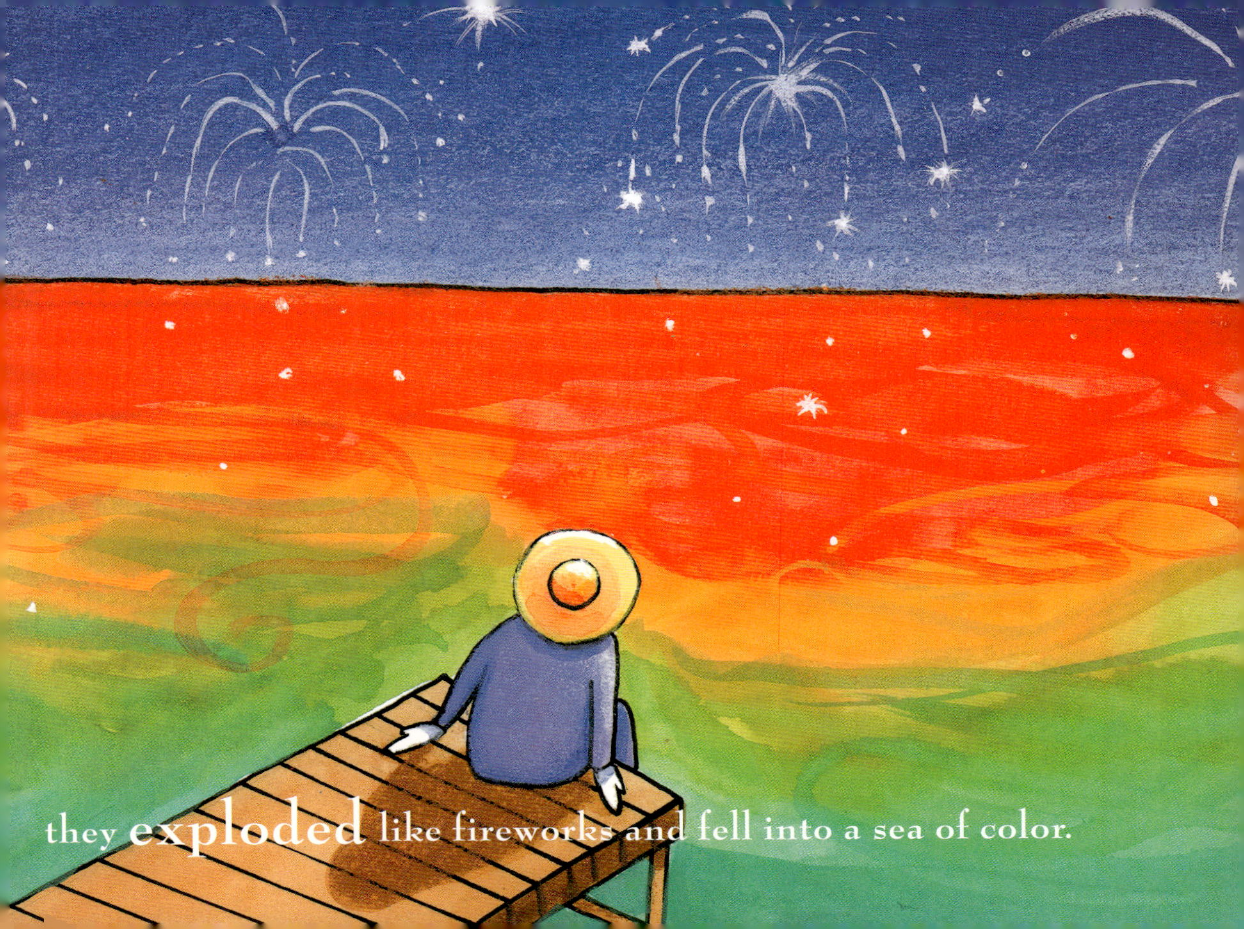

they **exploded** like fireworks and fell into a sea of color.

His Paint Box

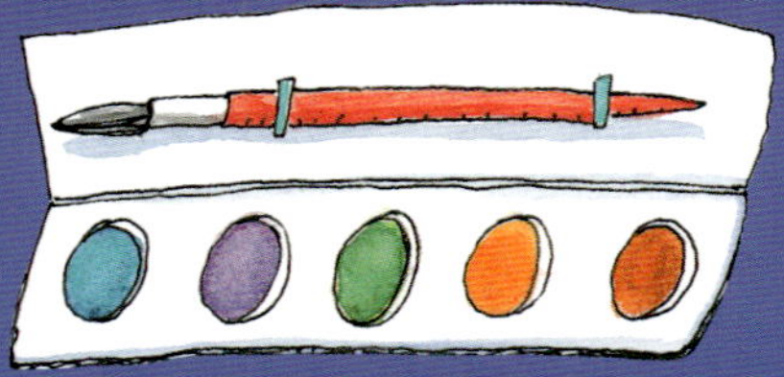

His paint box was full of many colors, the darkest of hues.

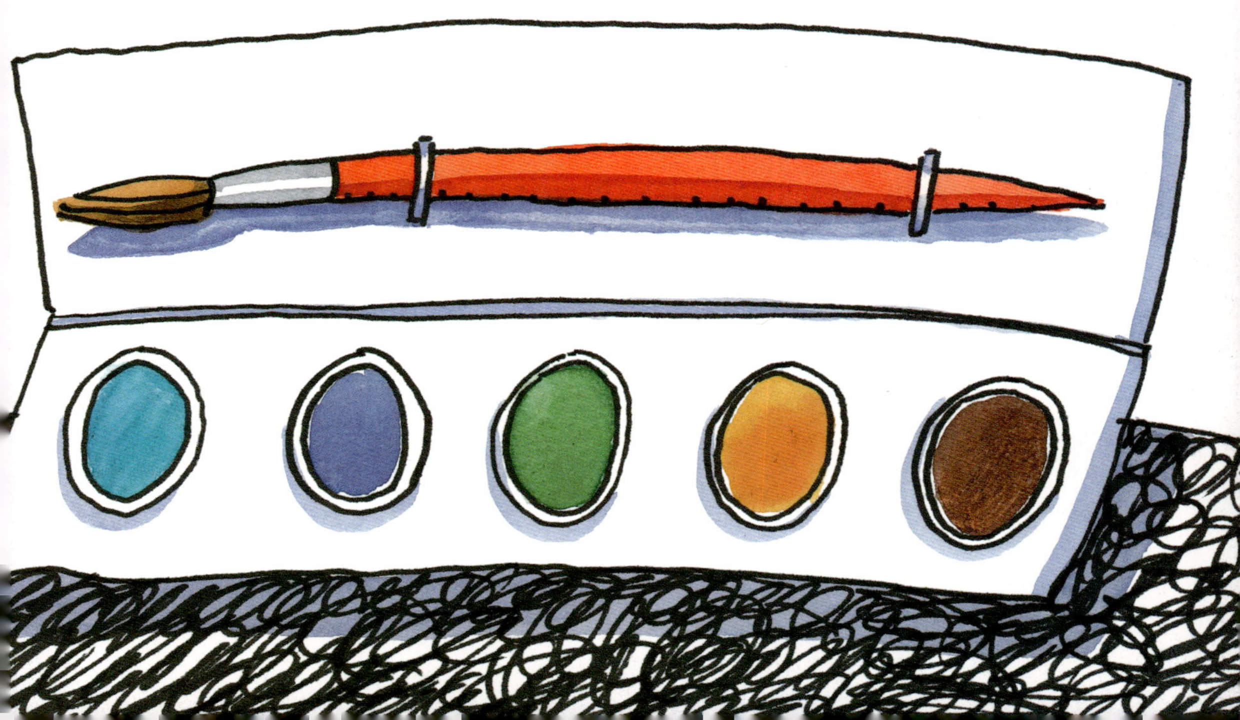

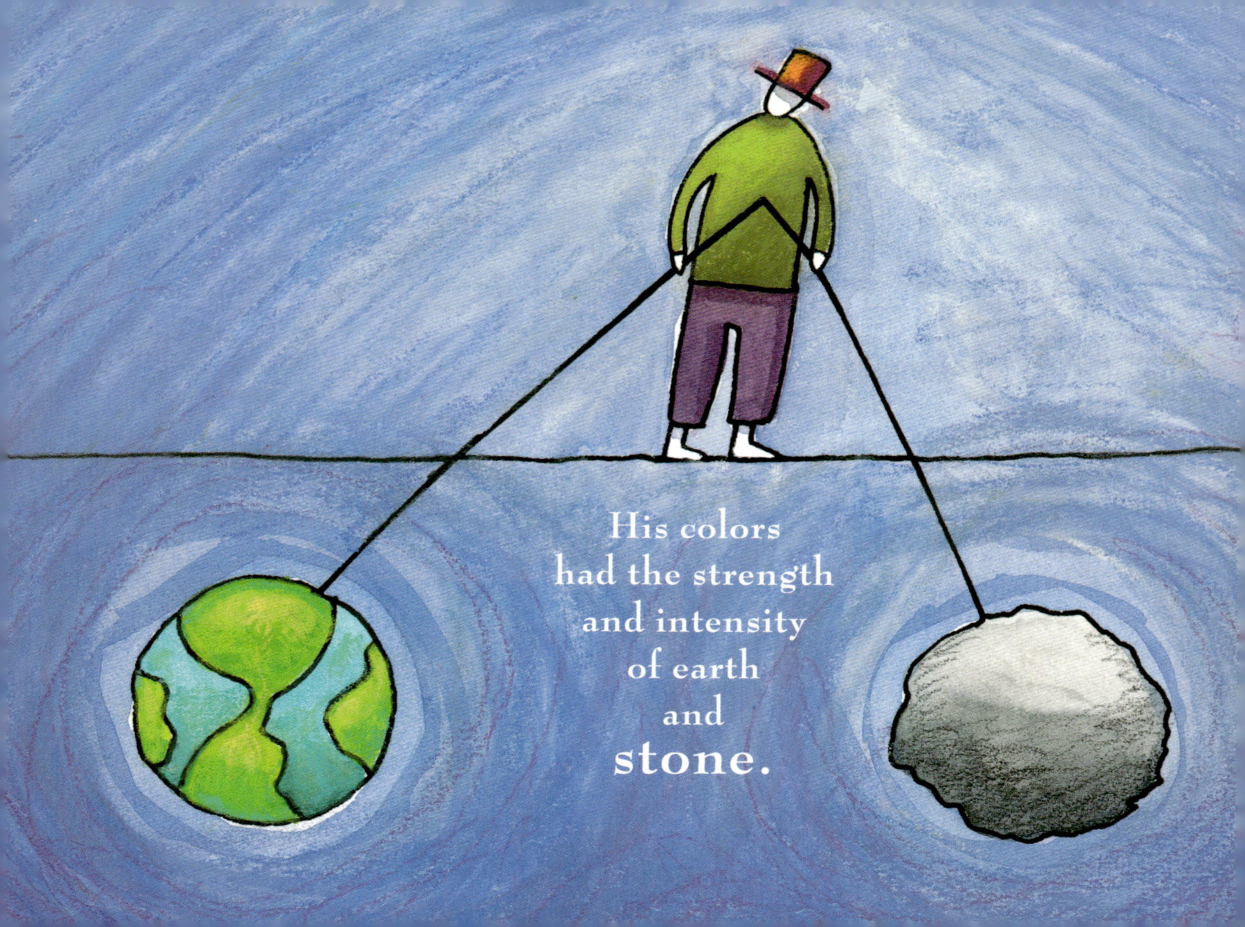

His colors
had the strength
and intensity
of earth
and
stone.

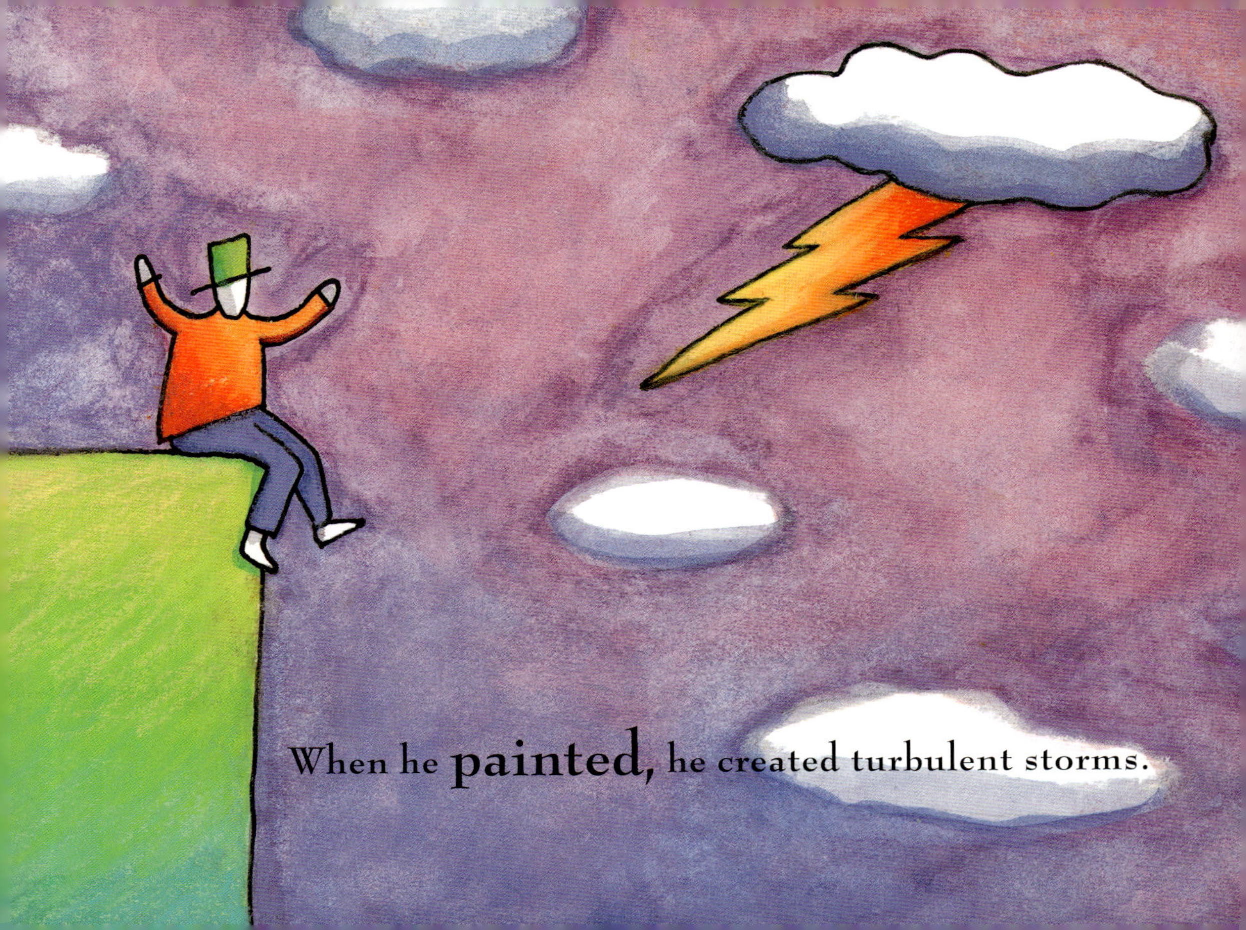

When he **painted,** he created turbulent storms.

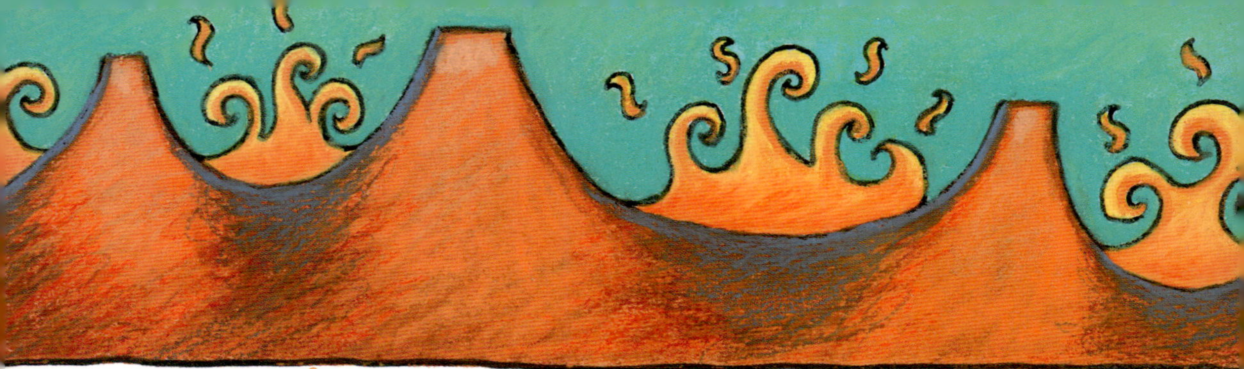

He painted fiery canyons

and the dense colors of the forest.

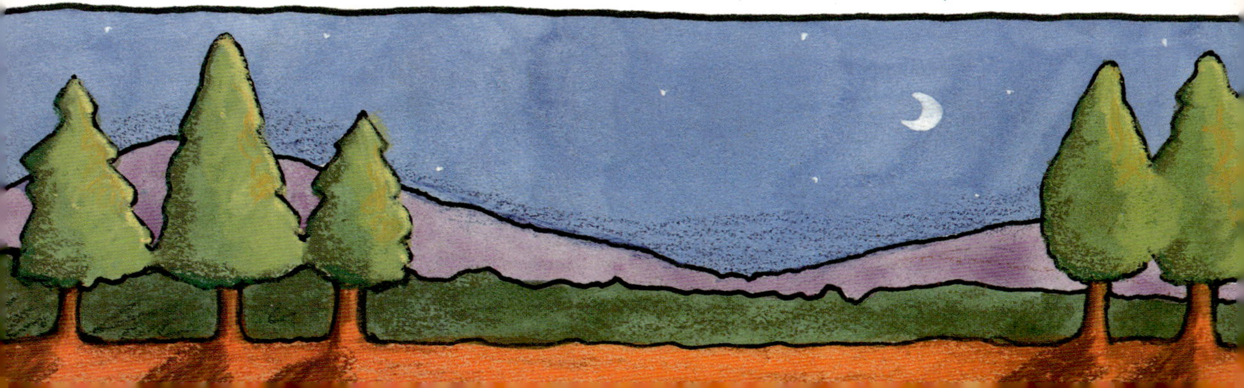

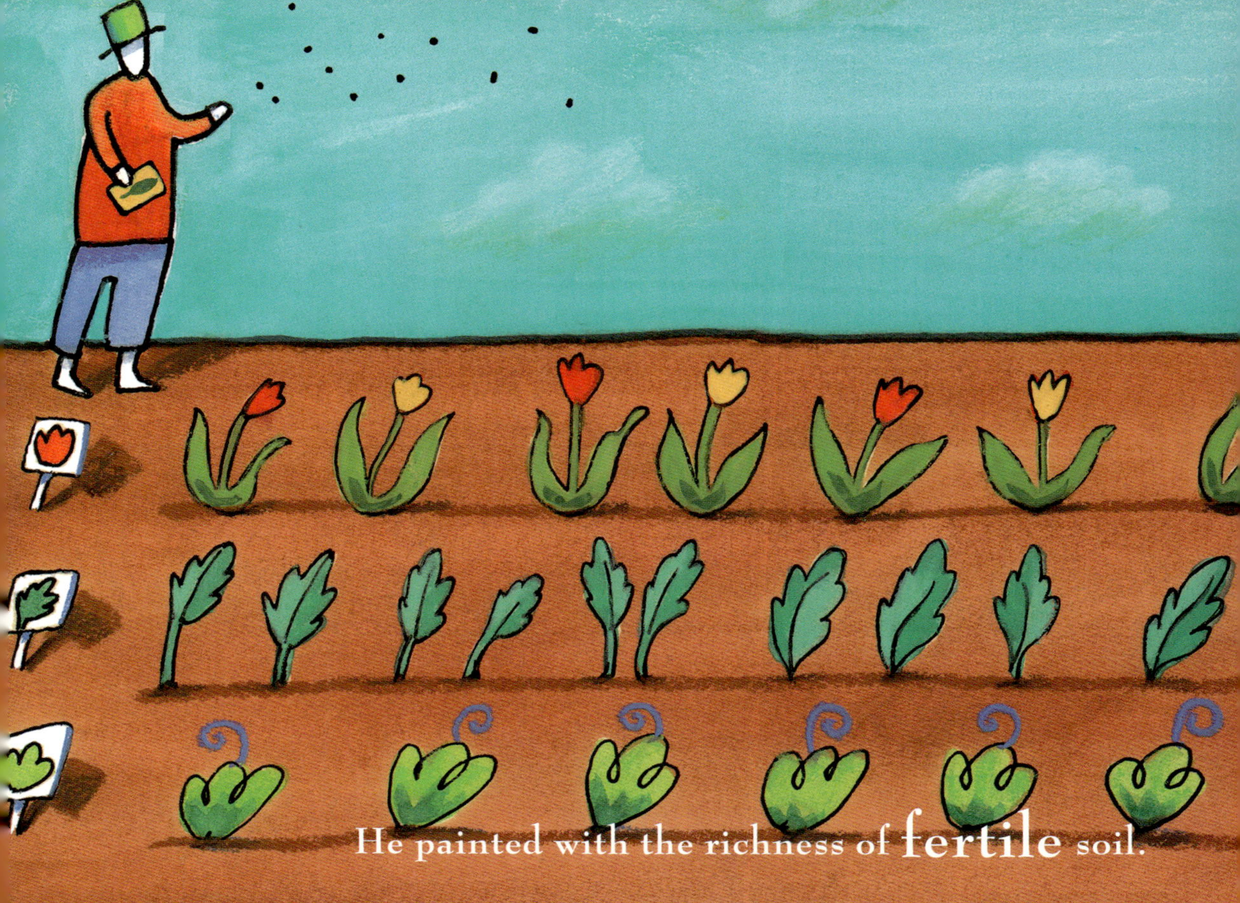

He painted with the richness of **fertile** soil.

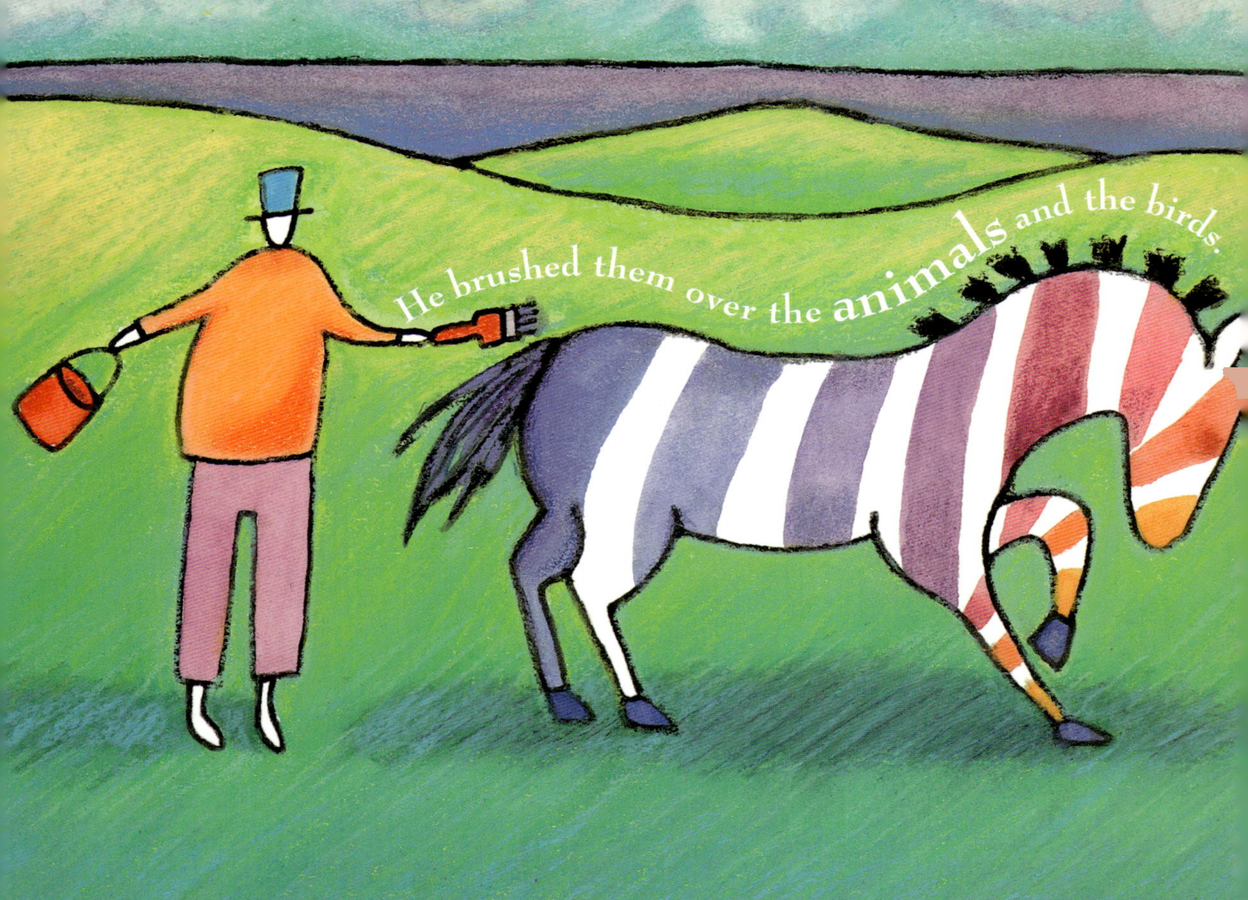
He brushed them over the animals and the birds.

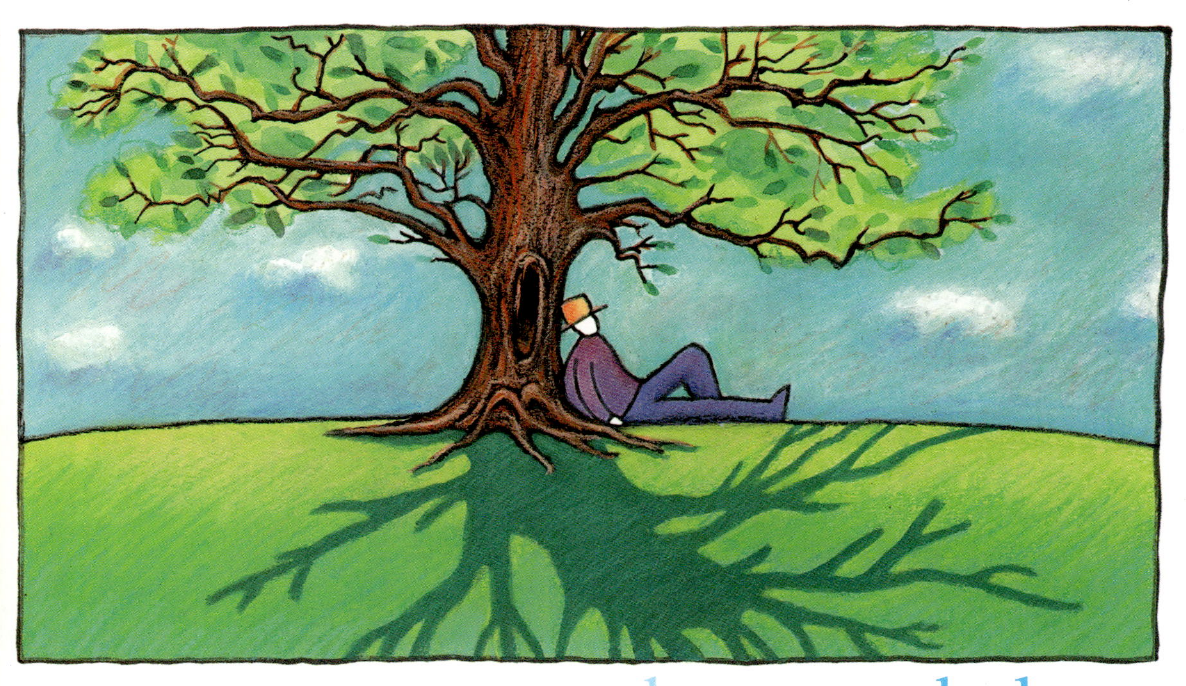

And he painted the cool summer shadows.

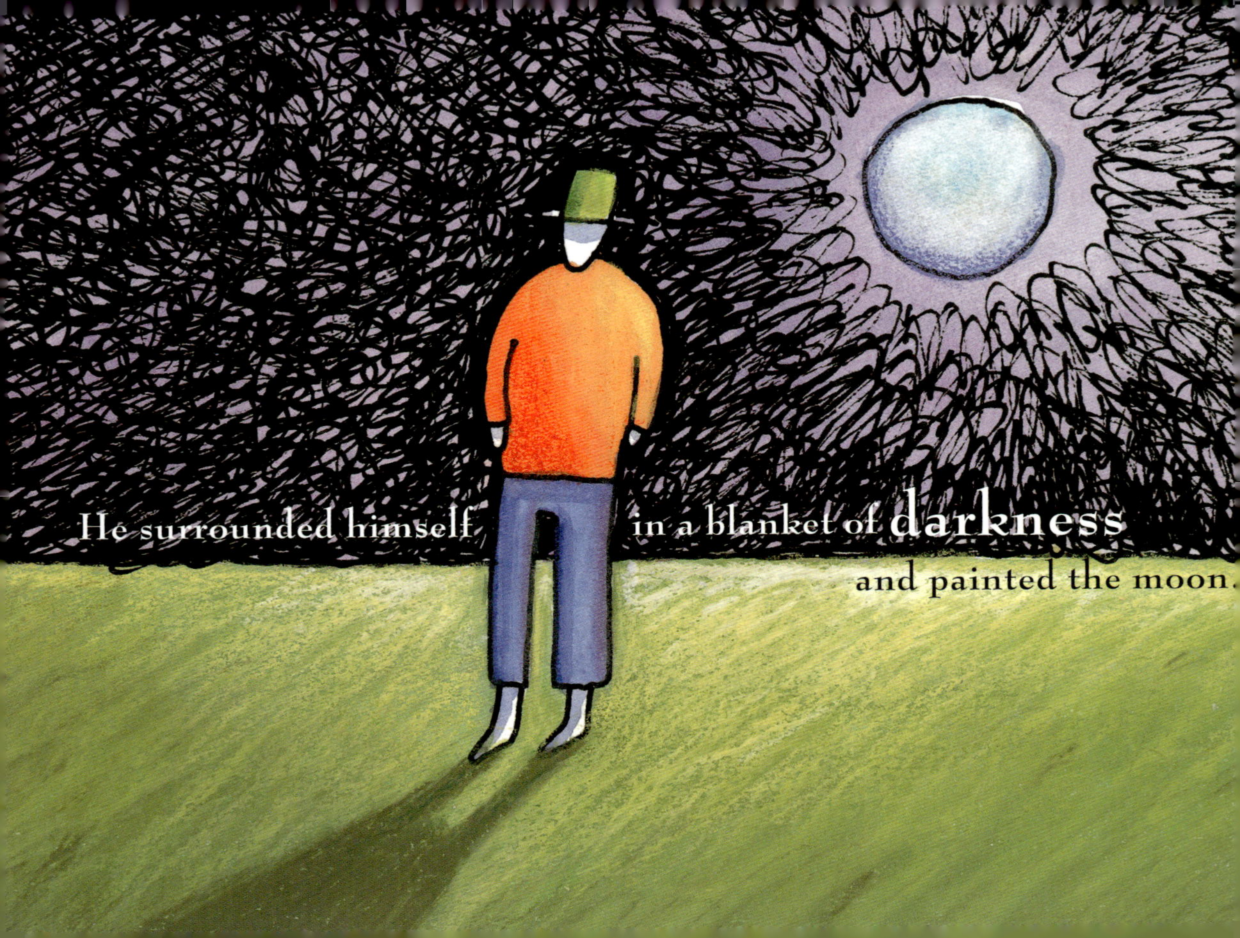
He surrounded himself in a blanket of darkness
and painted the moon.

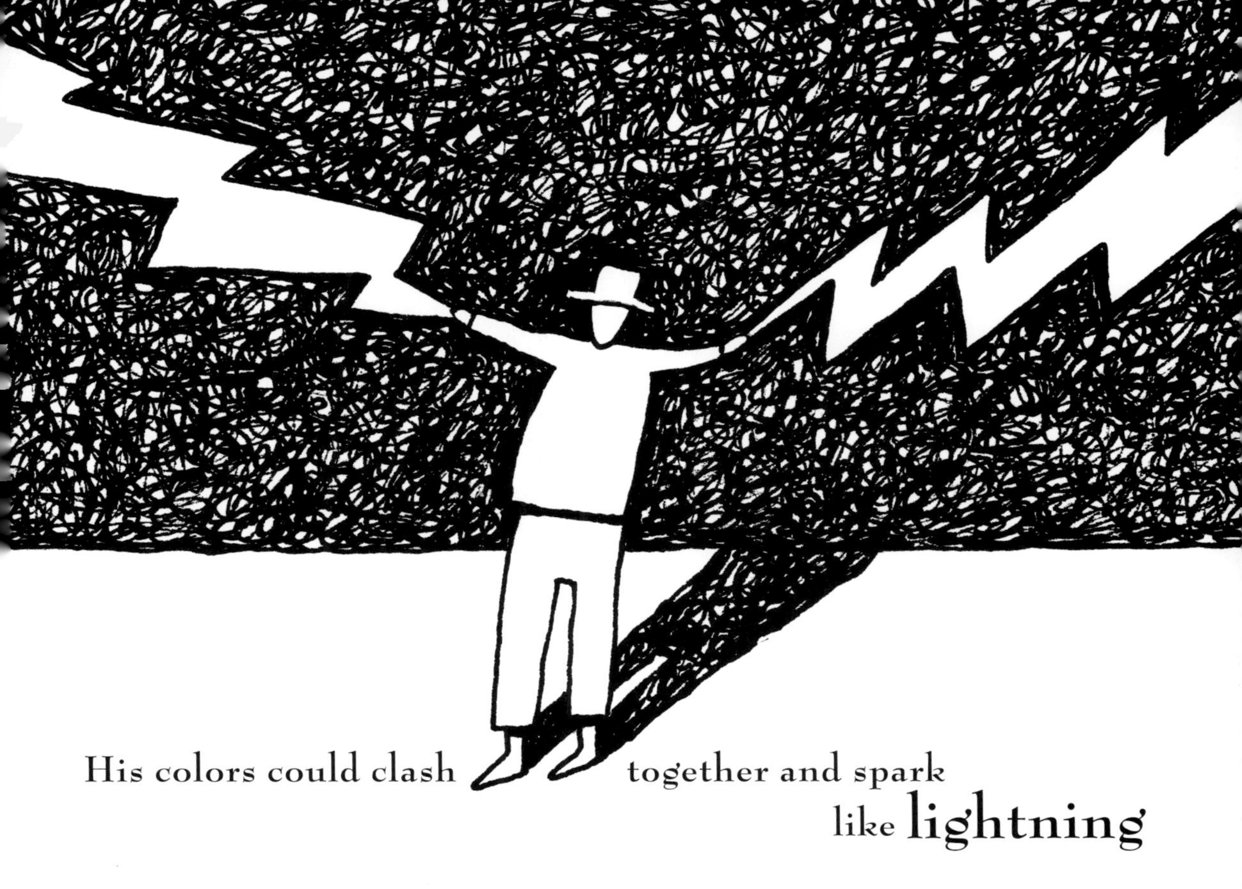

His colors could clash together and spark like **lightning**

or gently blow and rustle through the branches of the trees.

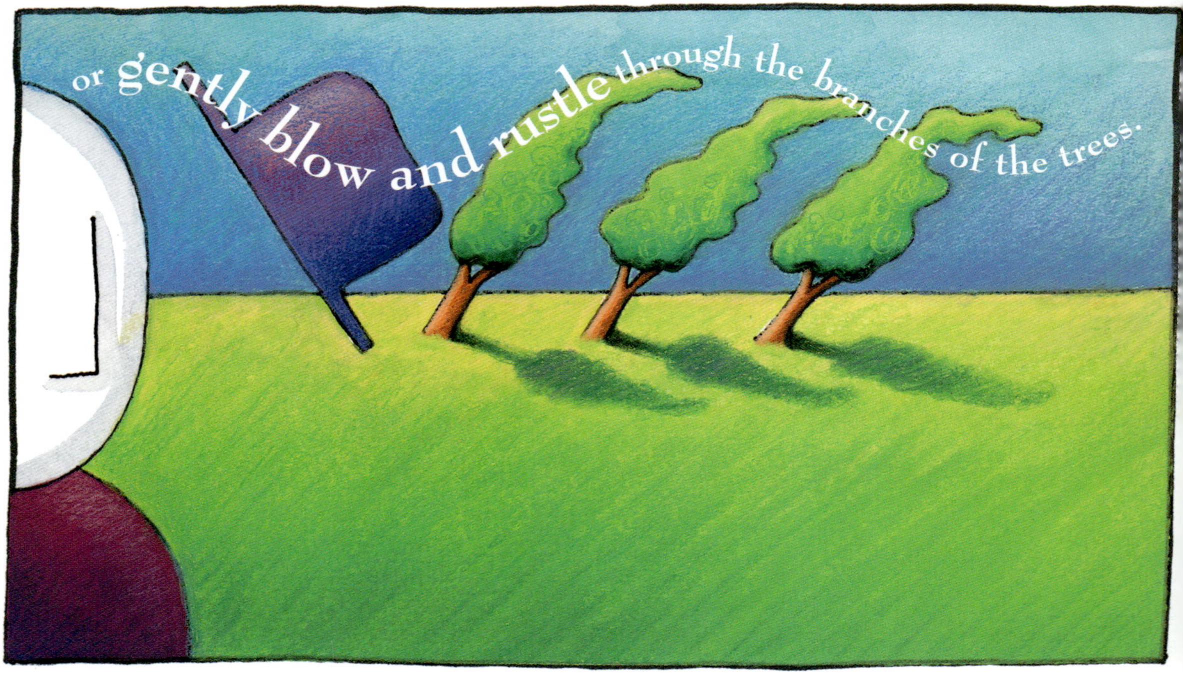

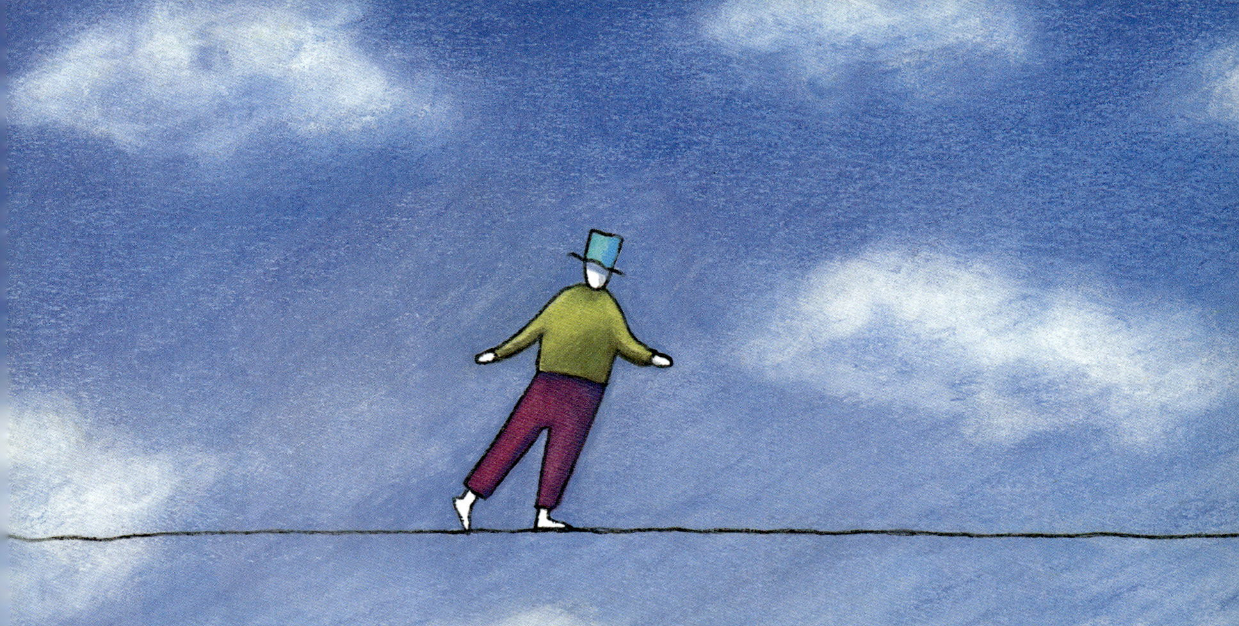

He painted
c a u t i o u s l y,

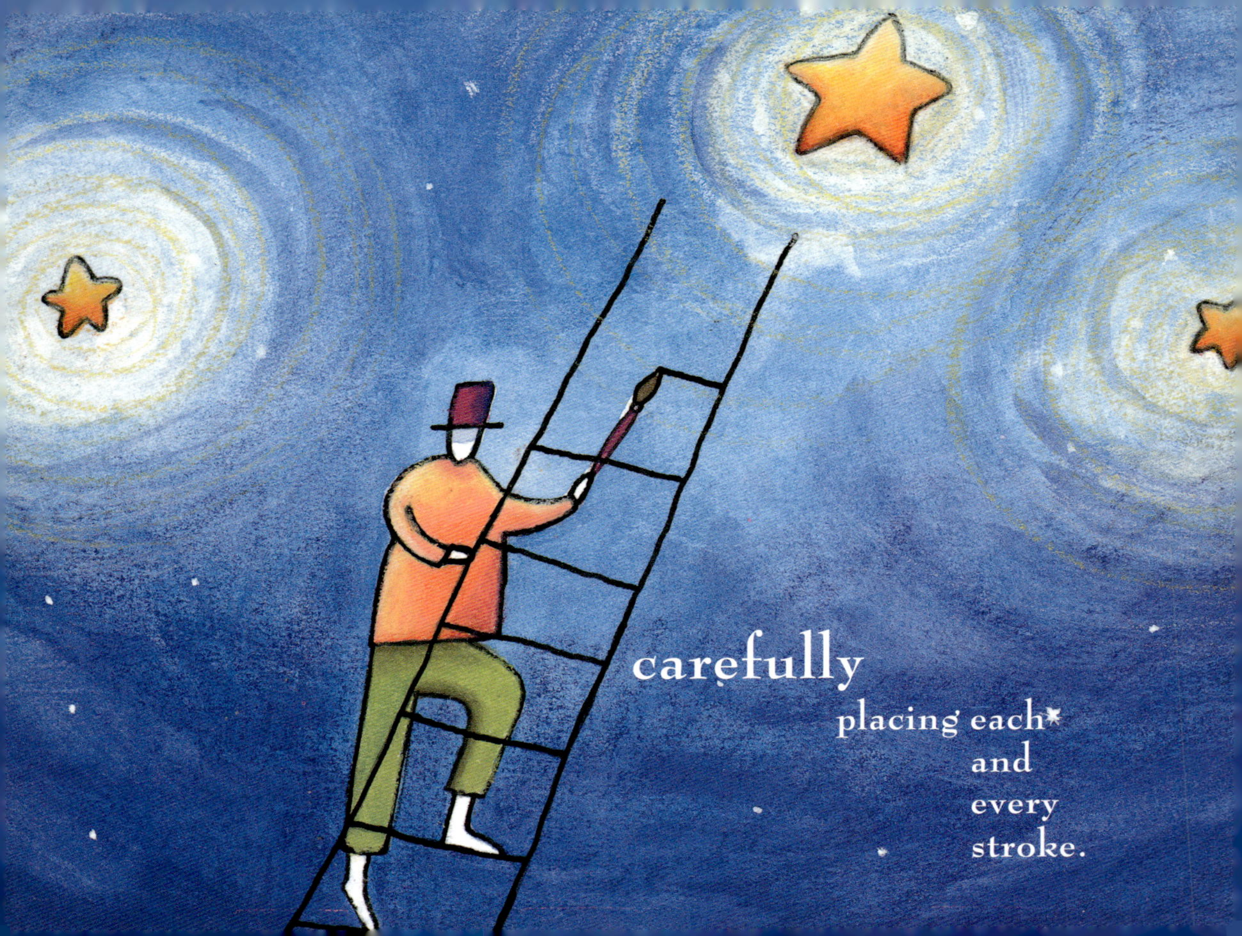
carefully
placing each
and
every
stroke.

His strokes were strong and **deliberate.**

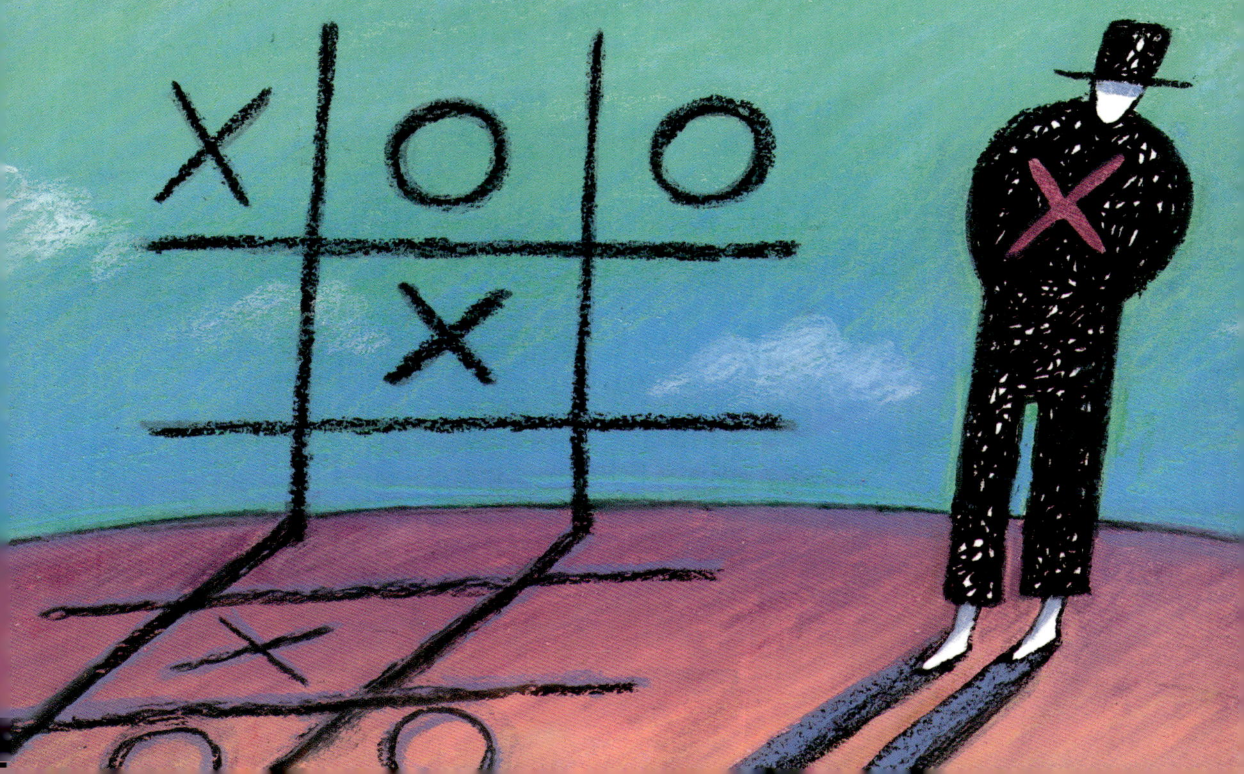

their Paint Box

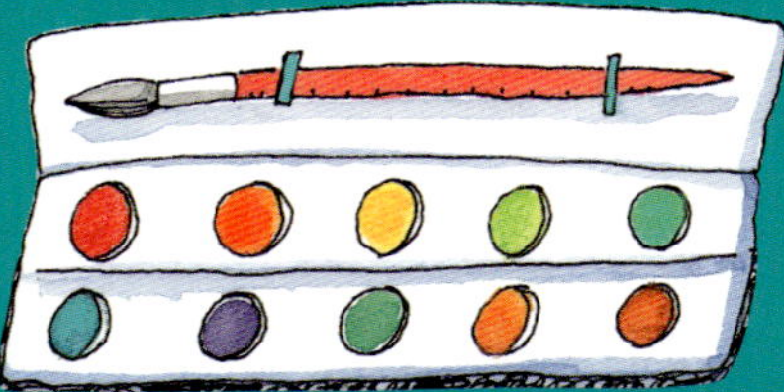

One day she was painting the sky to the ground

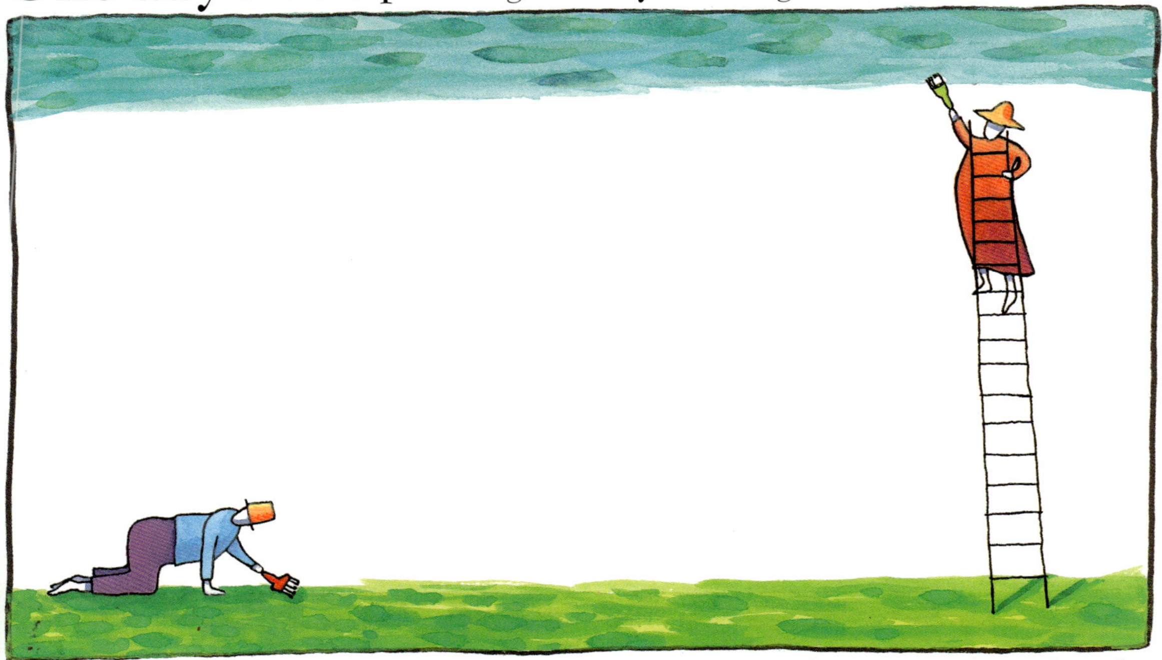

and he was painting the ground to the sky,

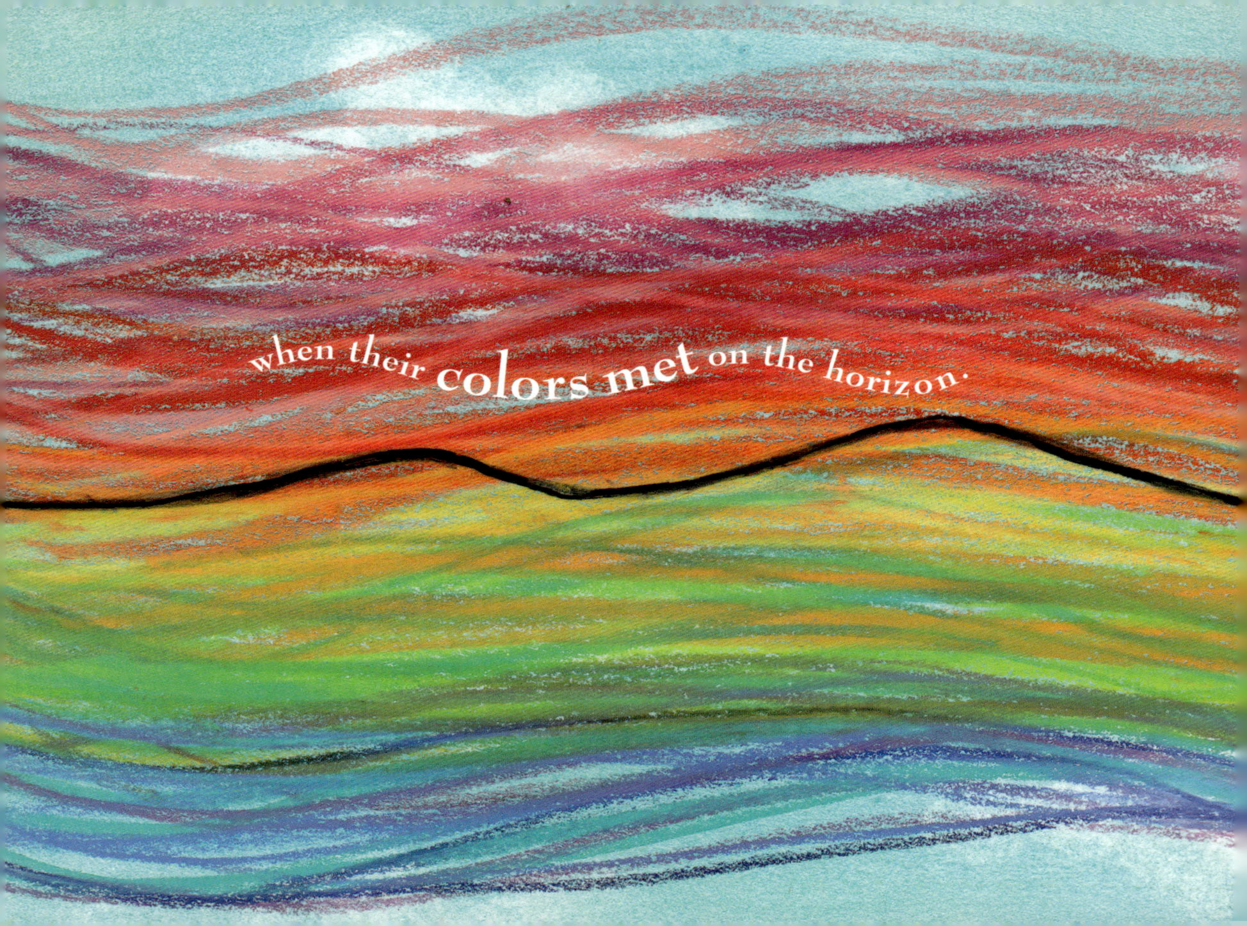

when their **colors met** on the horizon.

The paint ran together and danced and swirled

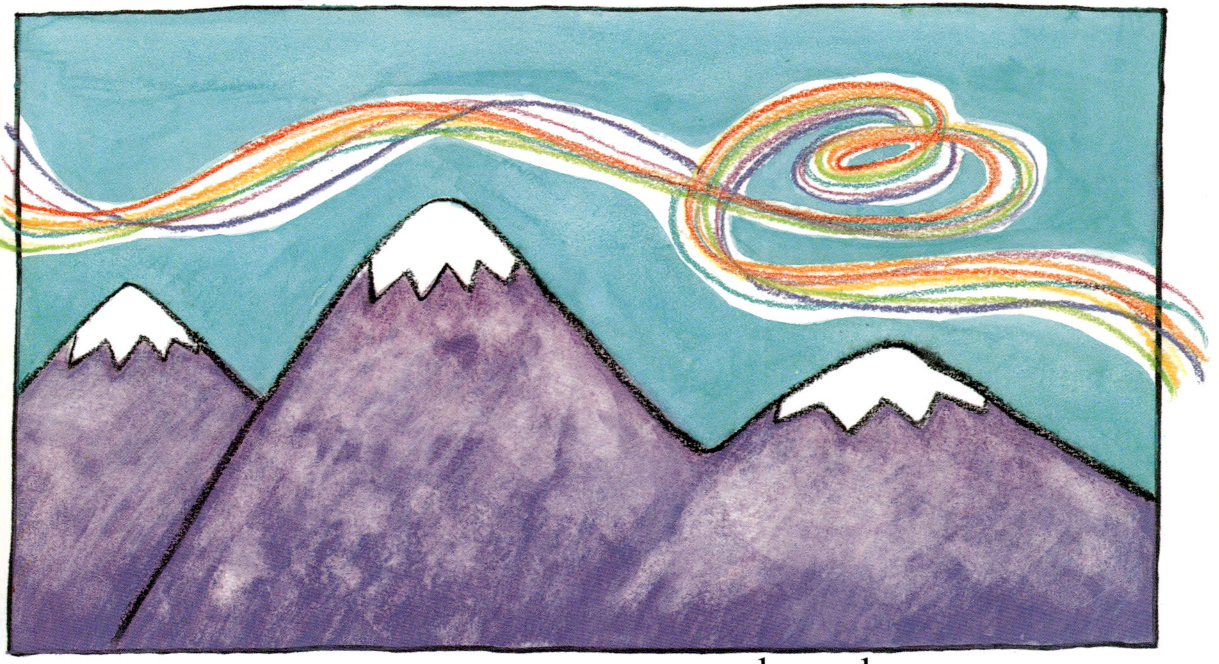

above the mountaintops.

It **blended** into the ocean.

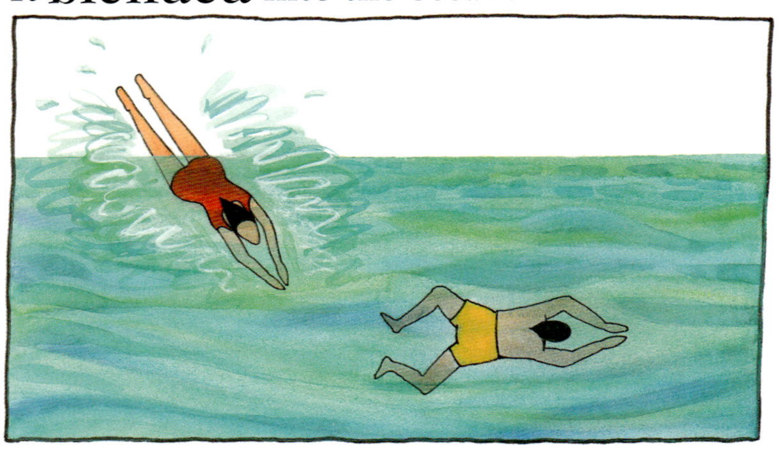

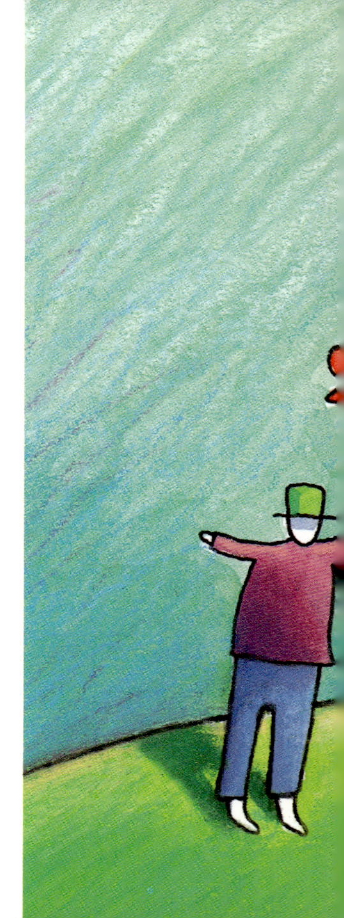

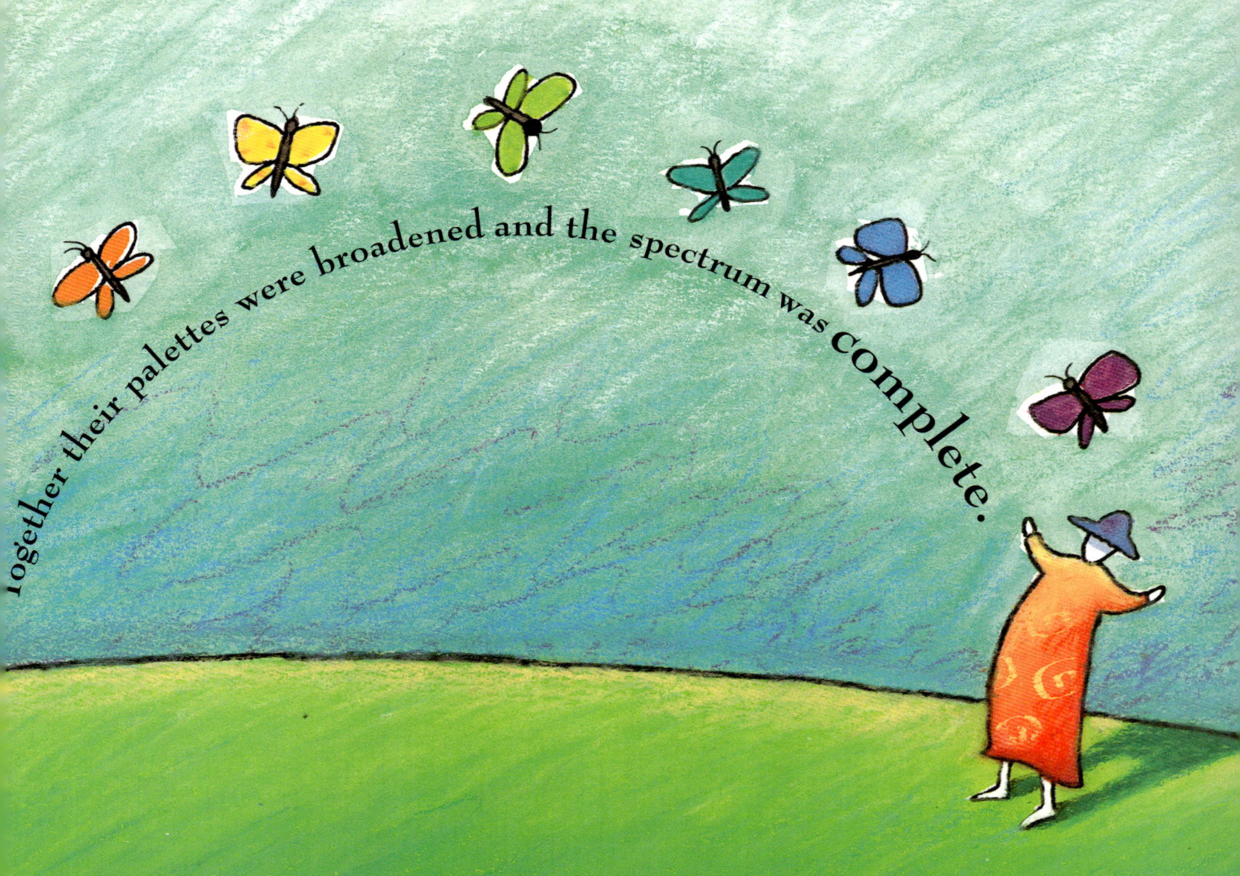

Together their palettes were broadened and the spectrum was **complete.**

Now they blissfully painted the world **together**

on one broad canvas.

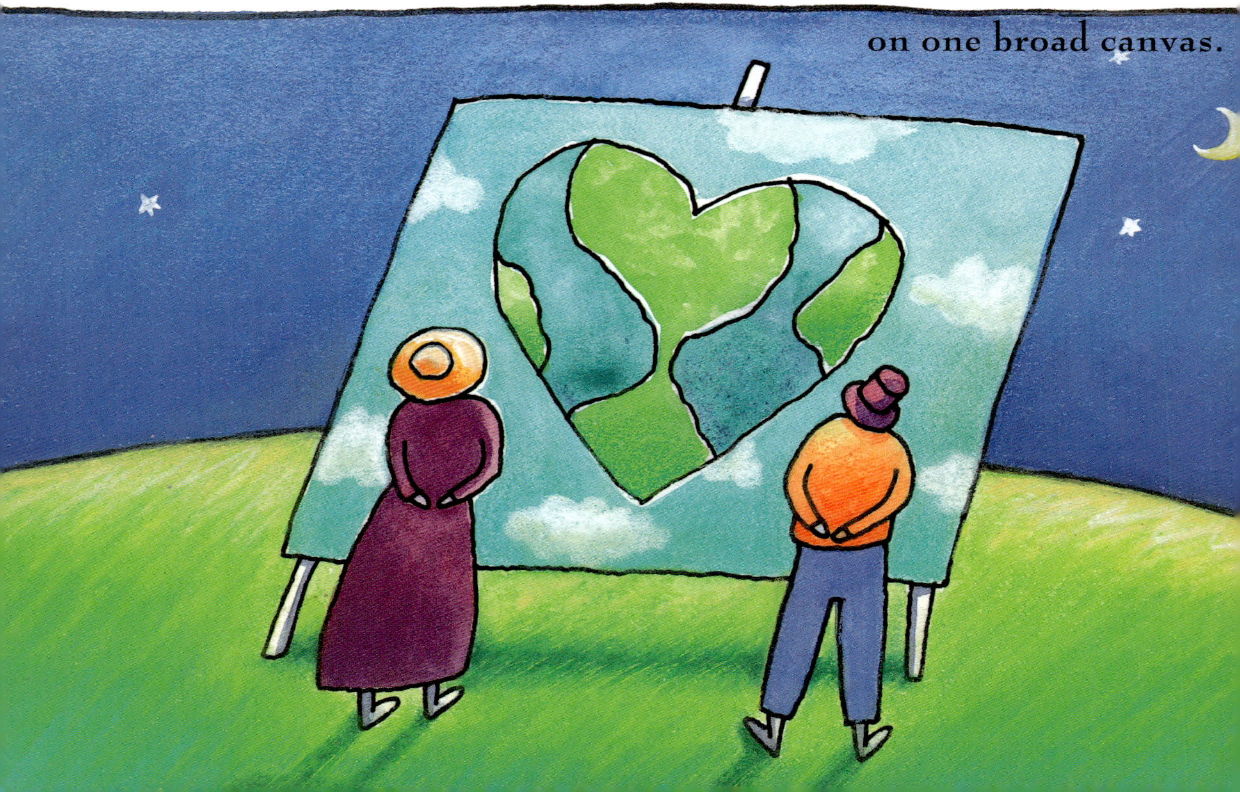

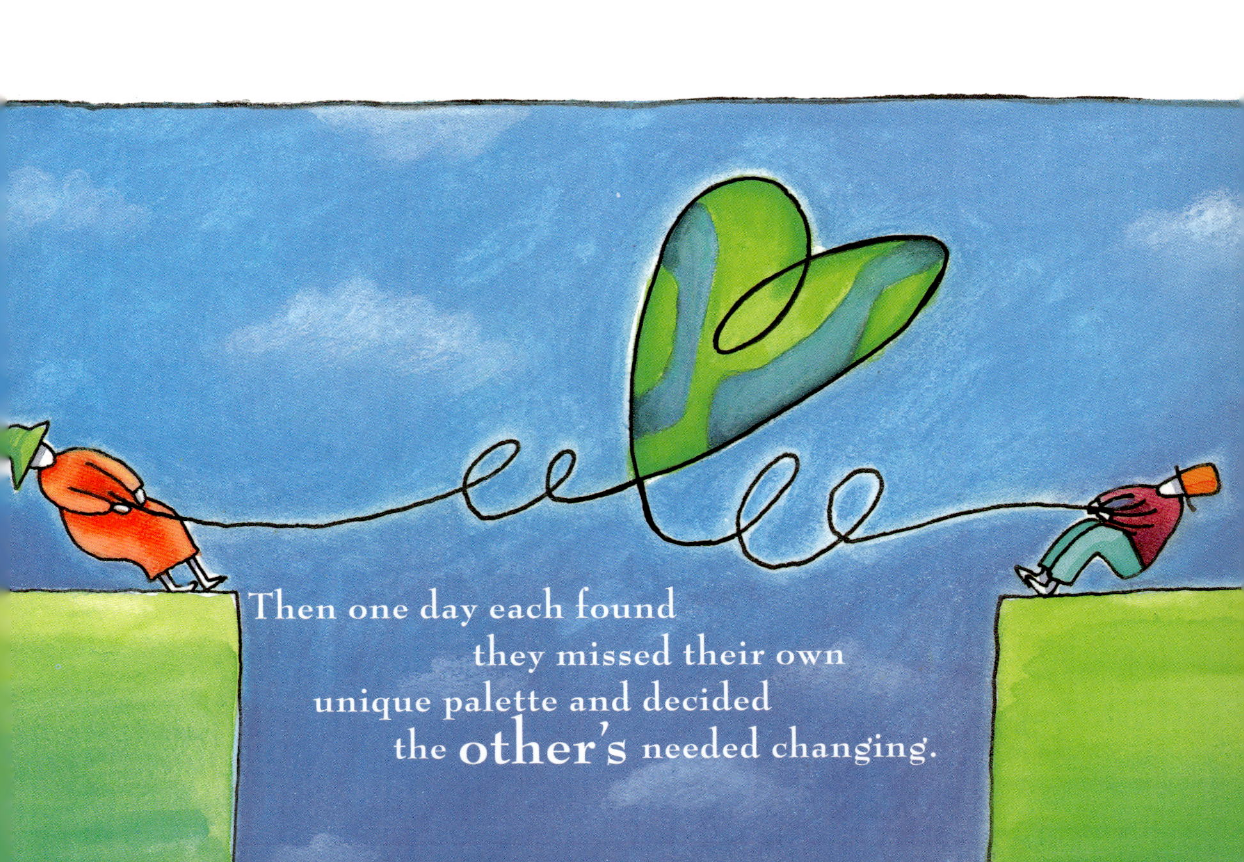

Then one day each found
they missed their own
unique palette and decided
the **other's** needed changing.

She scrubbed
and painted
furiously
to lighten
his dark colors.

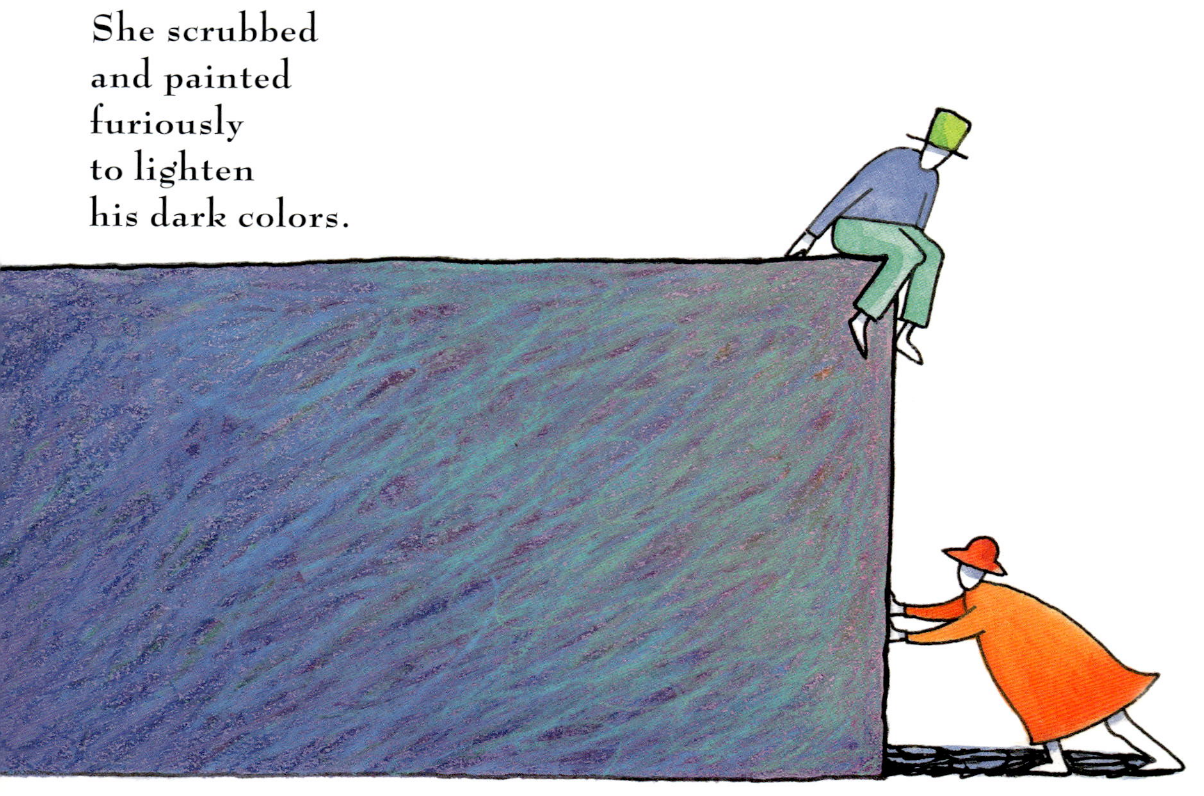

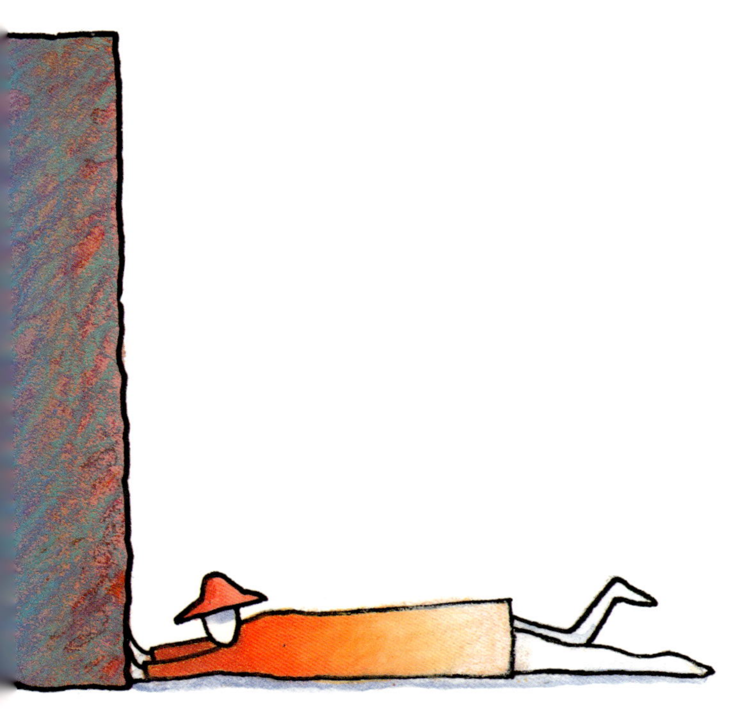

She added
more
and more
pigment
and mixed
her colors
with his
until her colors
were spent.

The harder she tried to **change** his colors,

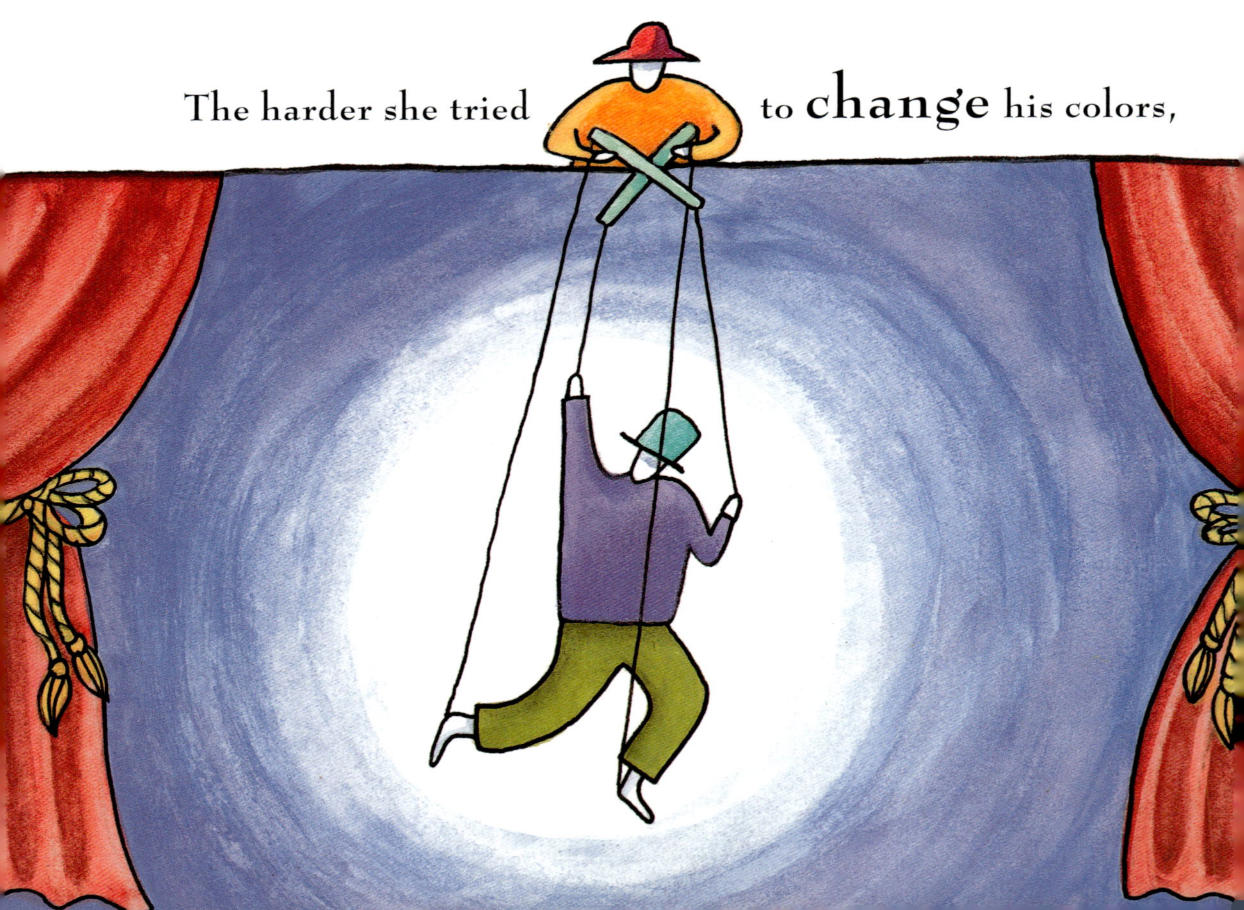

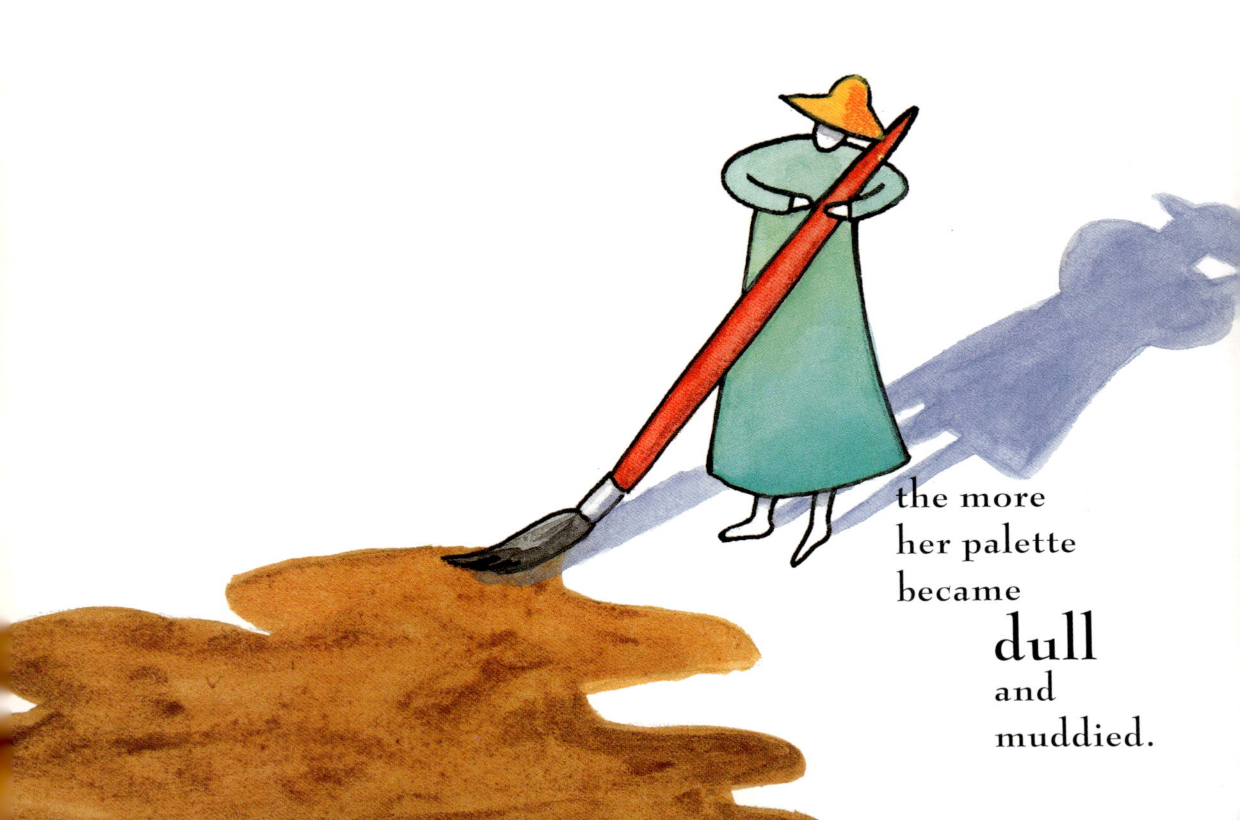

the more
her palette
became
dull
and
muddied.

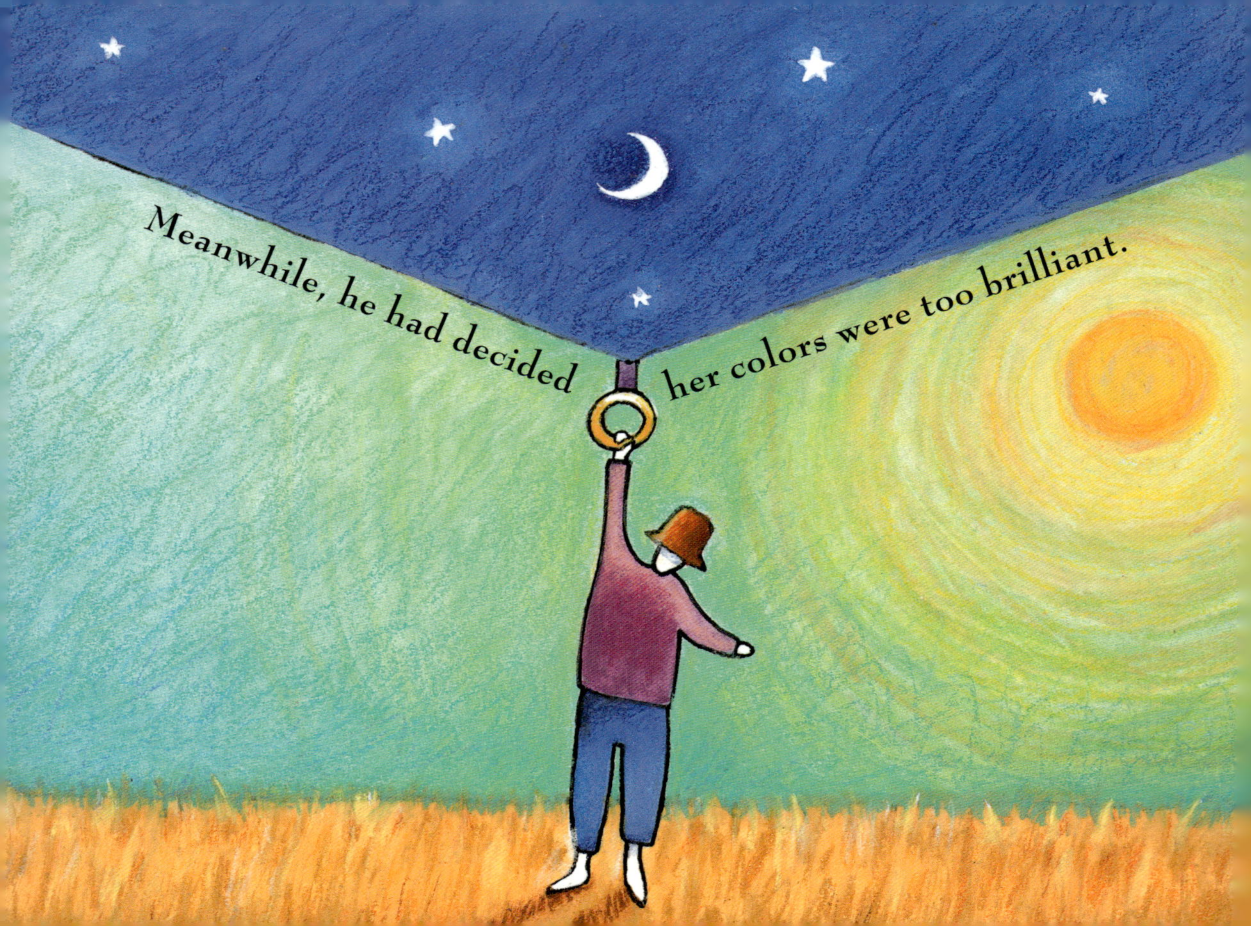

Meanwhile, he had decided her colors were too brilliant.

He tried unsuccessfully to paint his colors over hers.

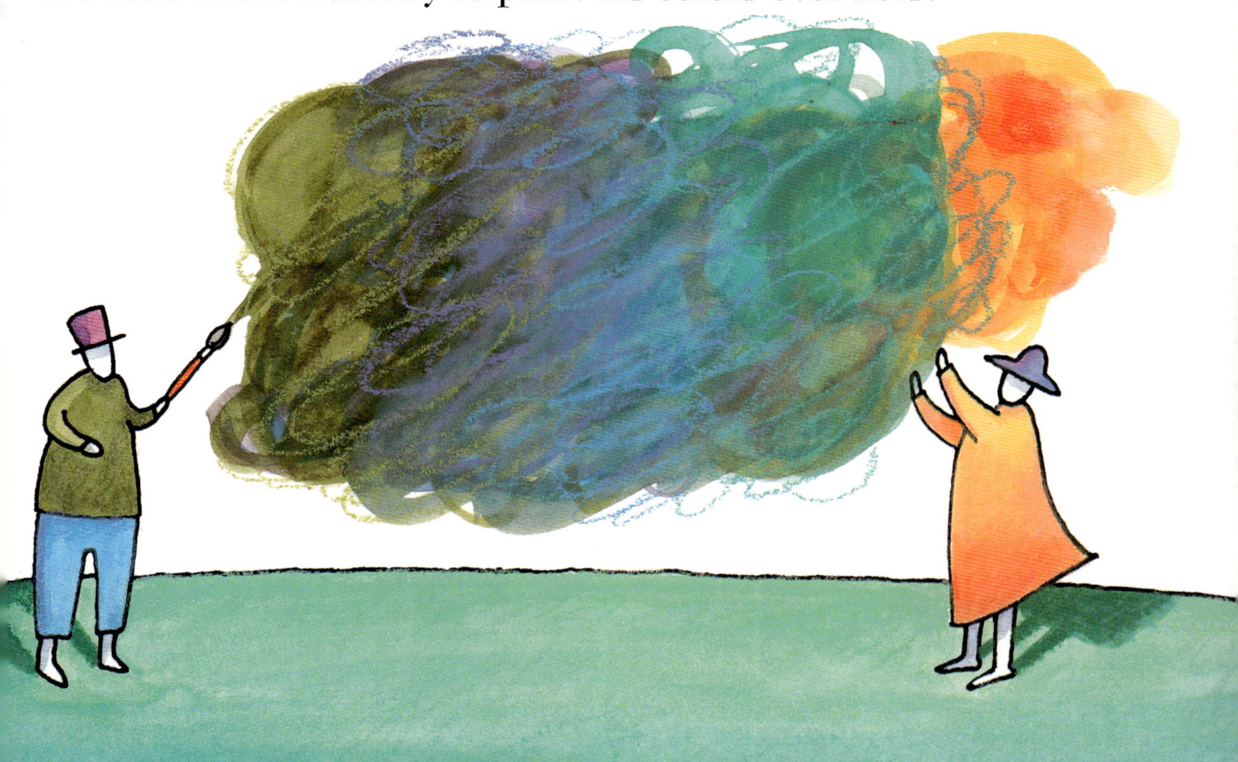

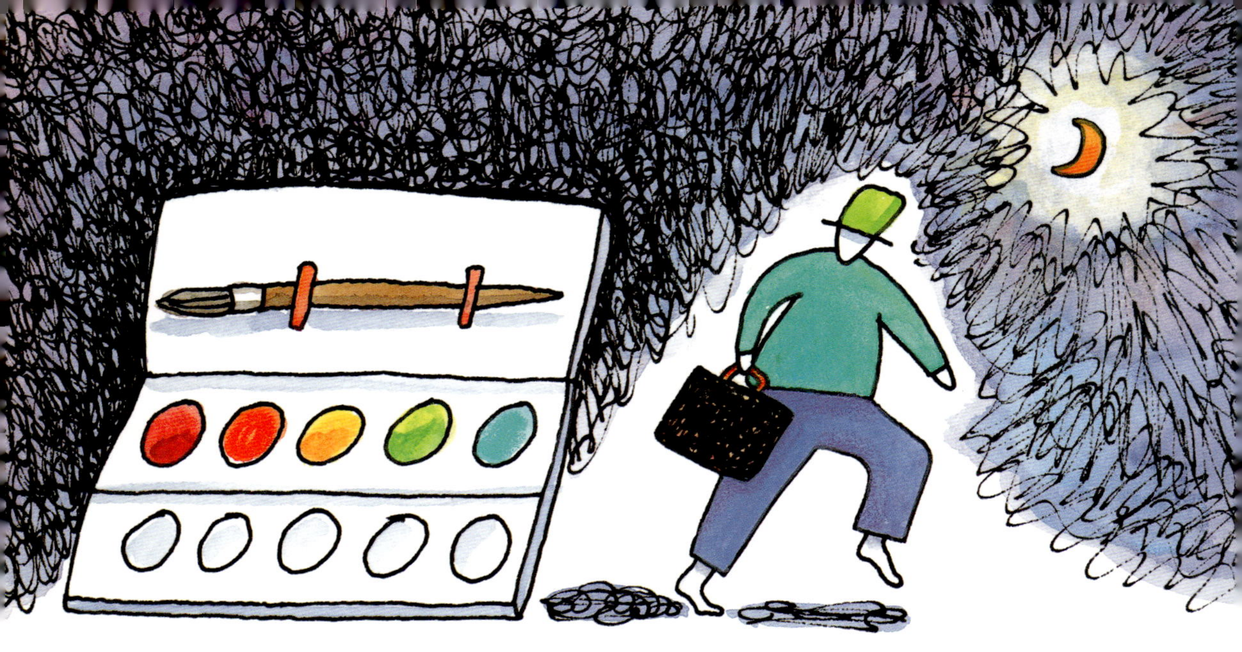

Then he carefully
tried to remove
his colors
from the box.

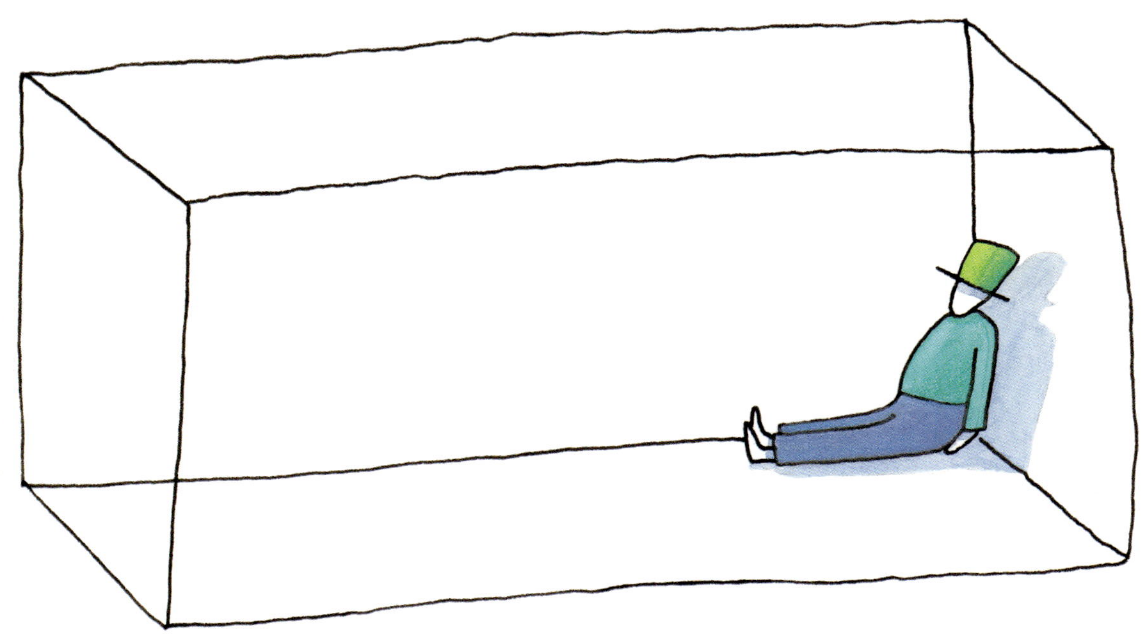

He regretted giving his colors so freely.

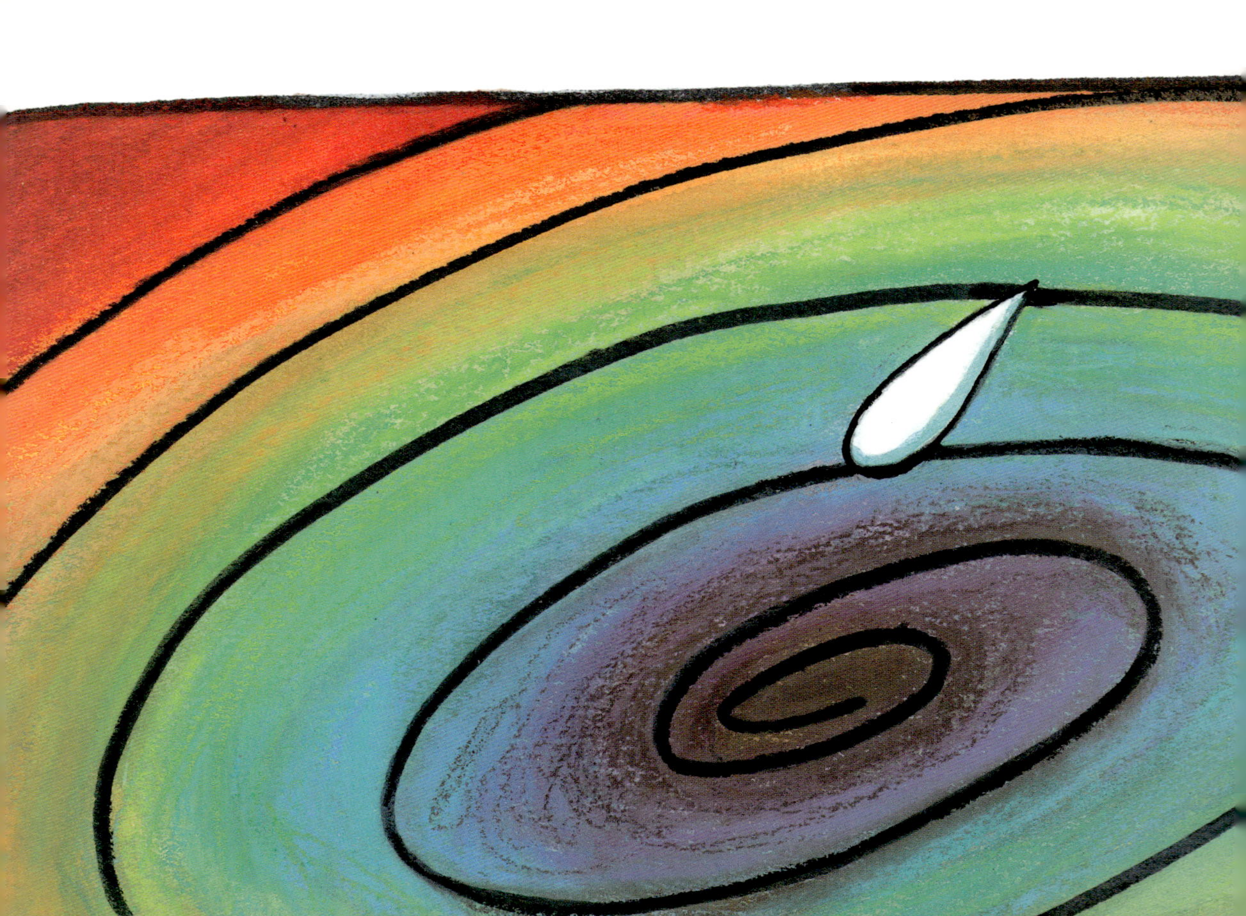

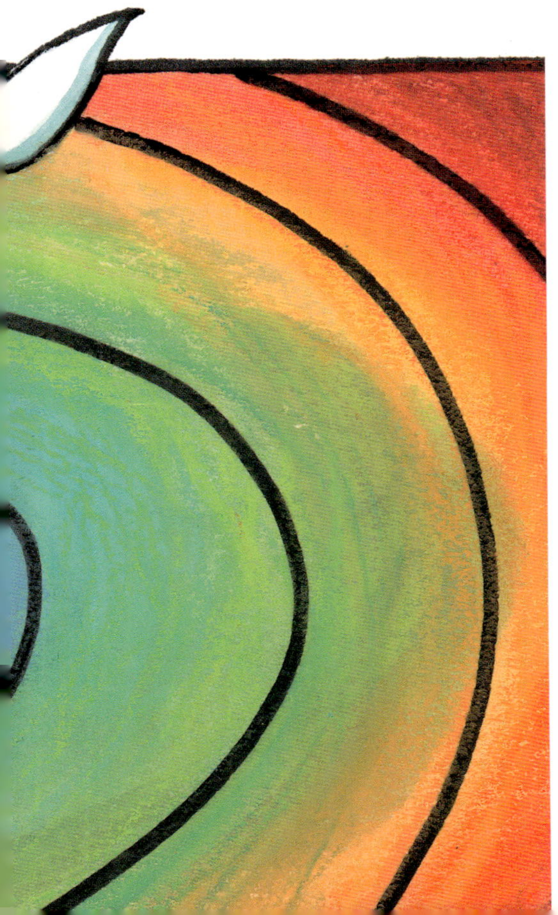

The thought
of losing their own
unique colors
made each of them
sad. Tears fell
into the palette
and swirled
around until they
were a muddy
brown.

They stared down
into the mixture
of their colors,

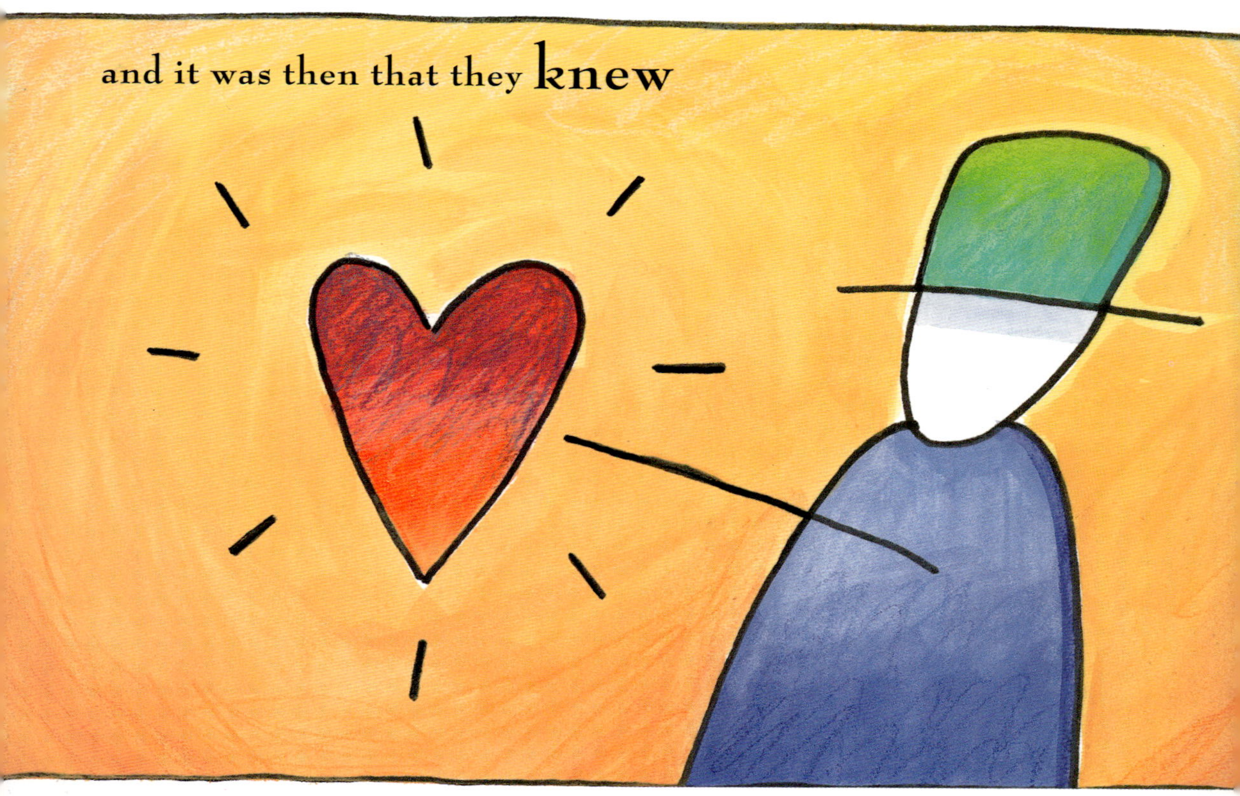
and it was then that they knew

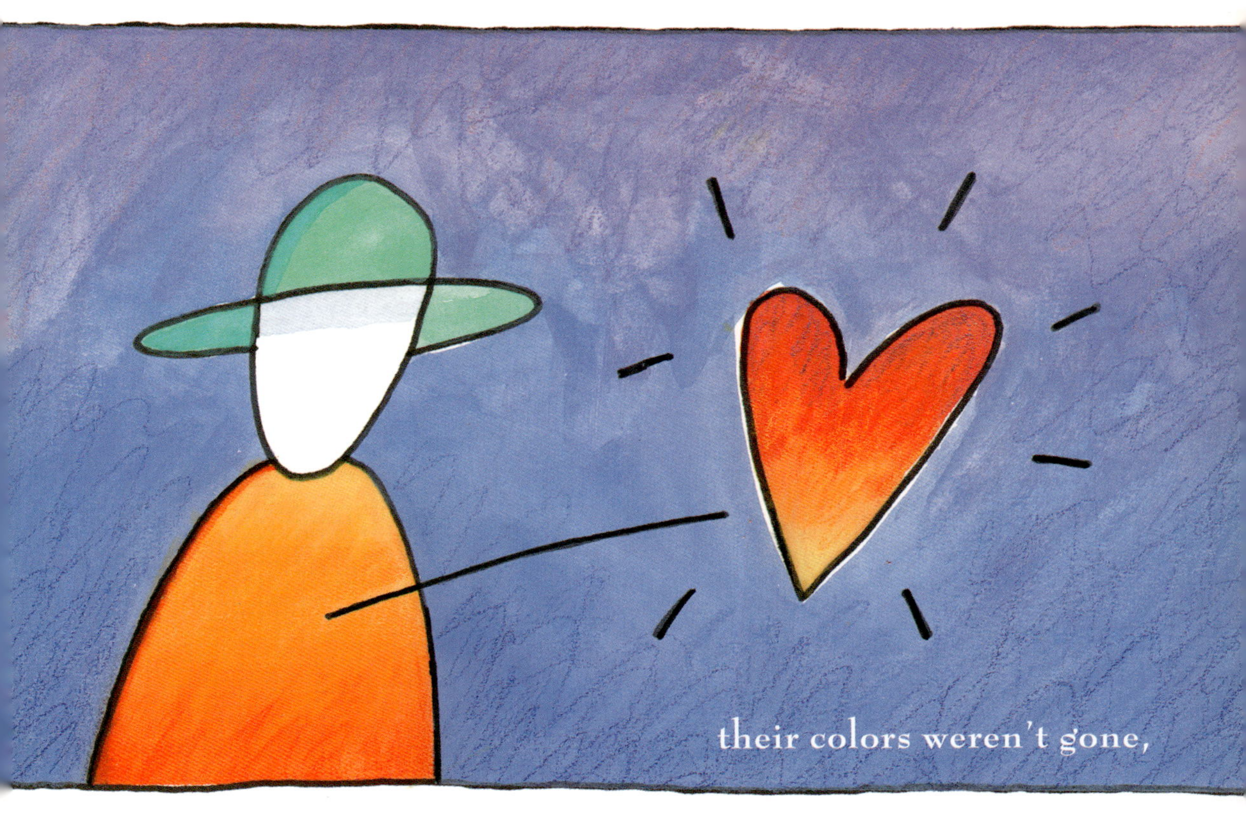

their colors weren't gone,

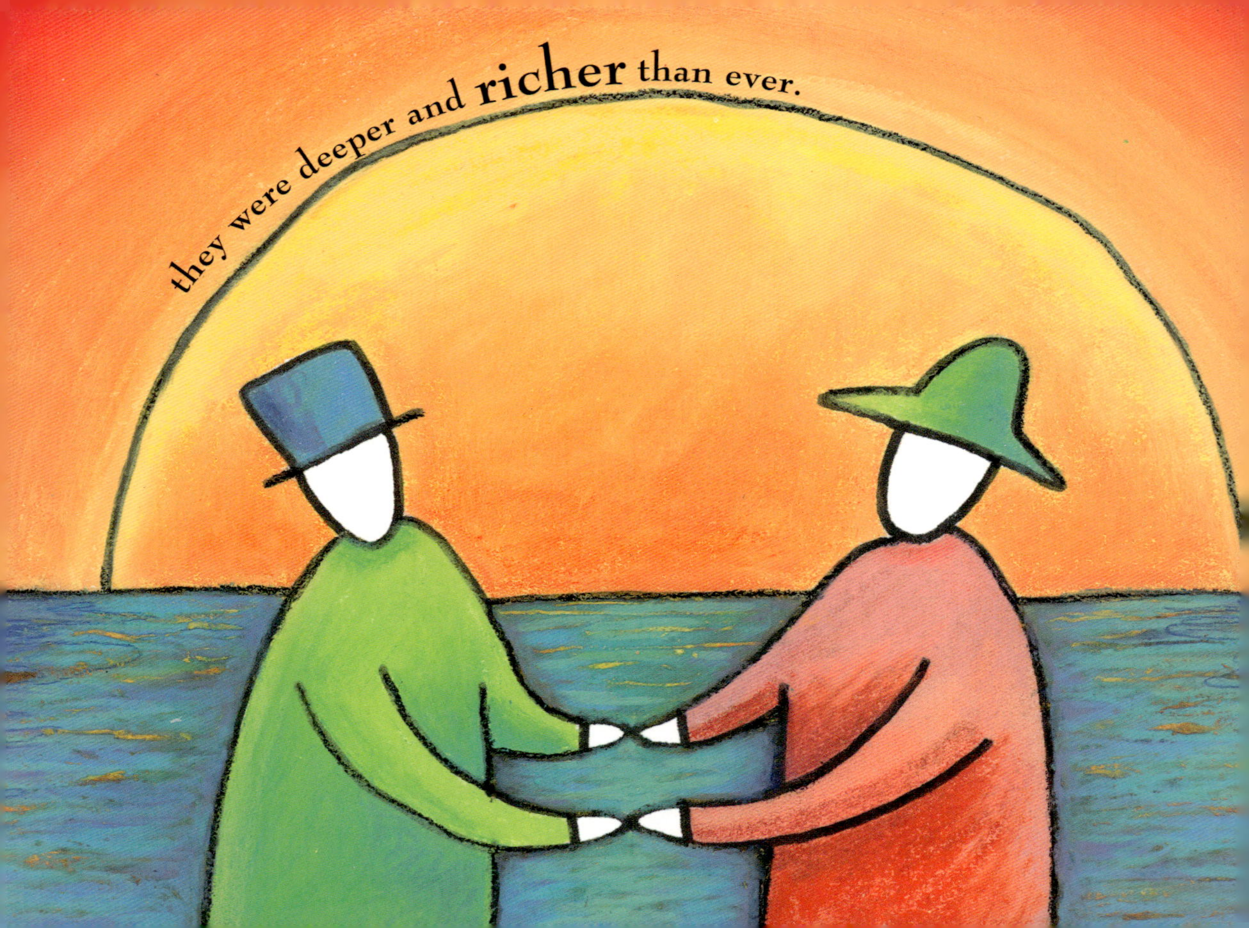

they were deeper and **richer** than ever.

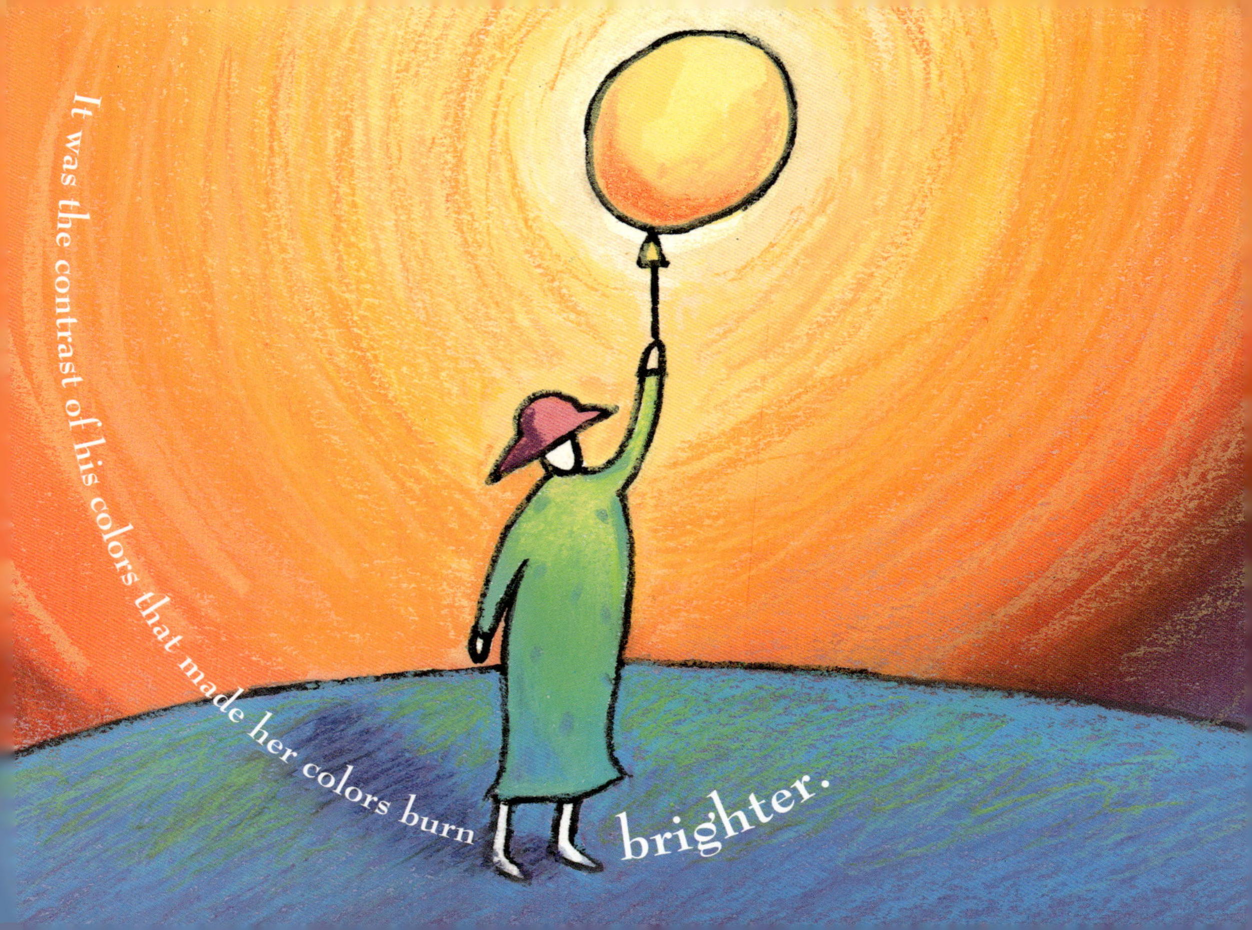

It was the contrast of his colors that made her colors burn **brighter.**

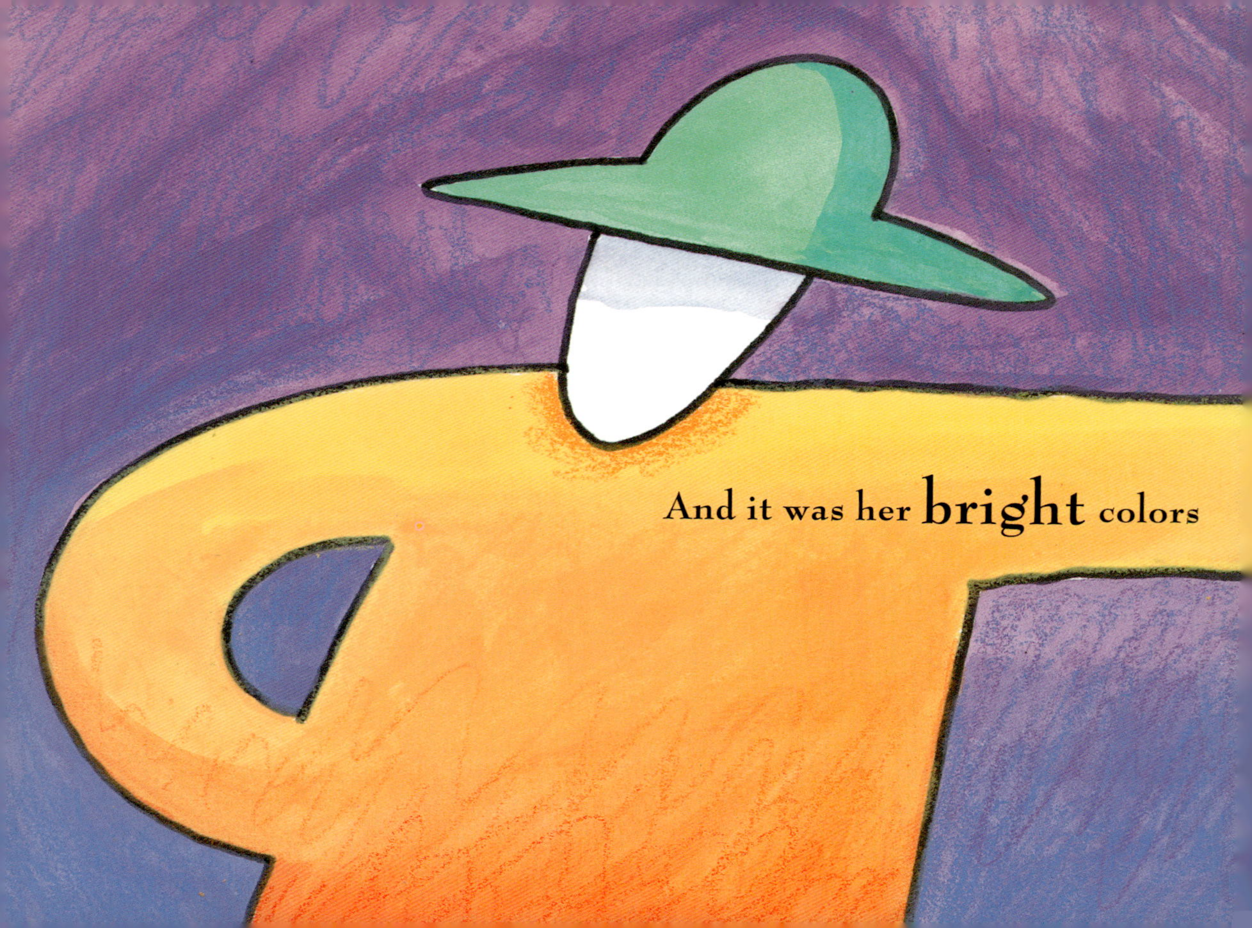

And it was her **bright** colors

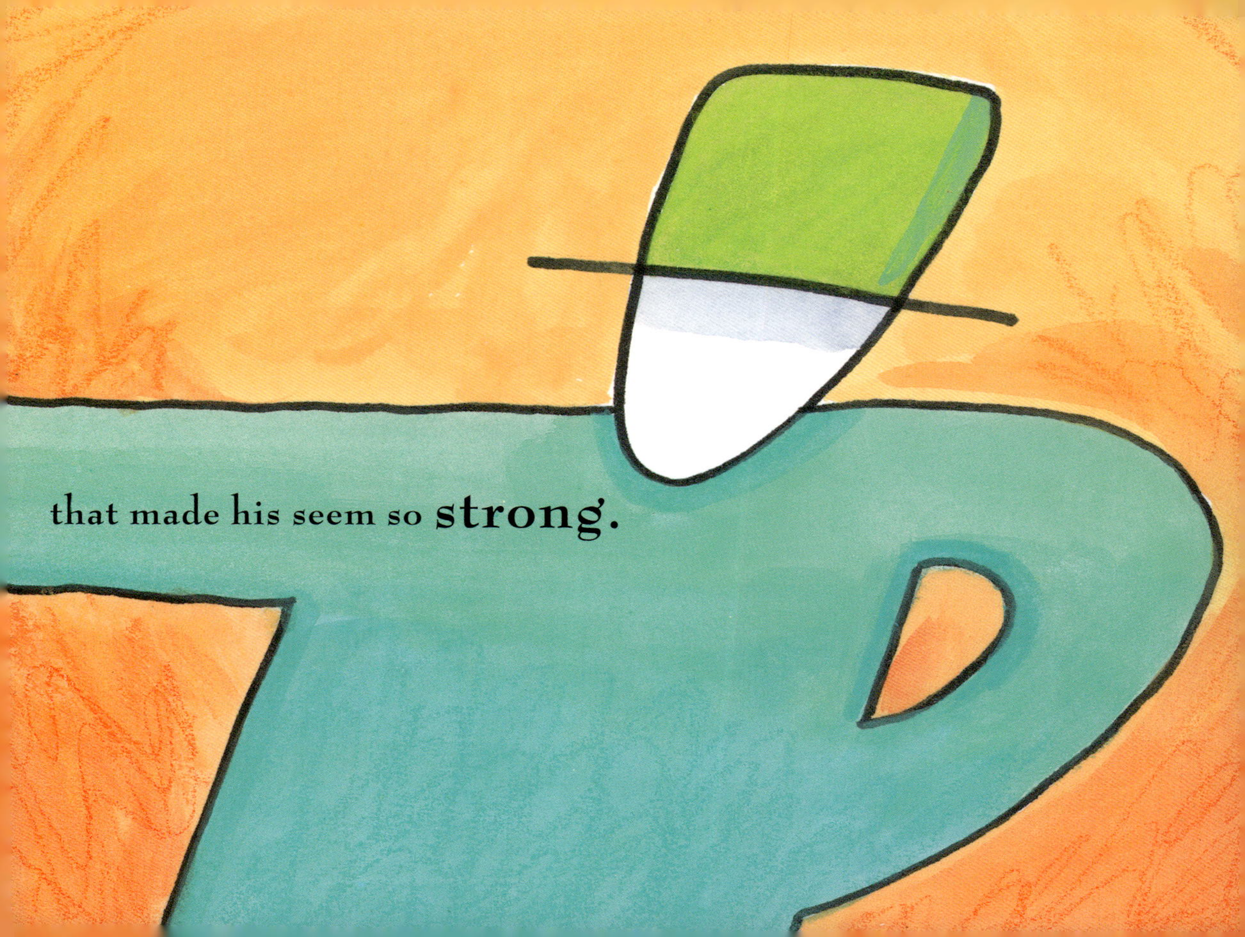

that made his seem so **strong.**

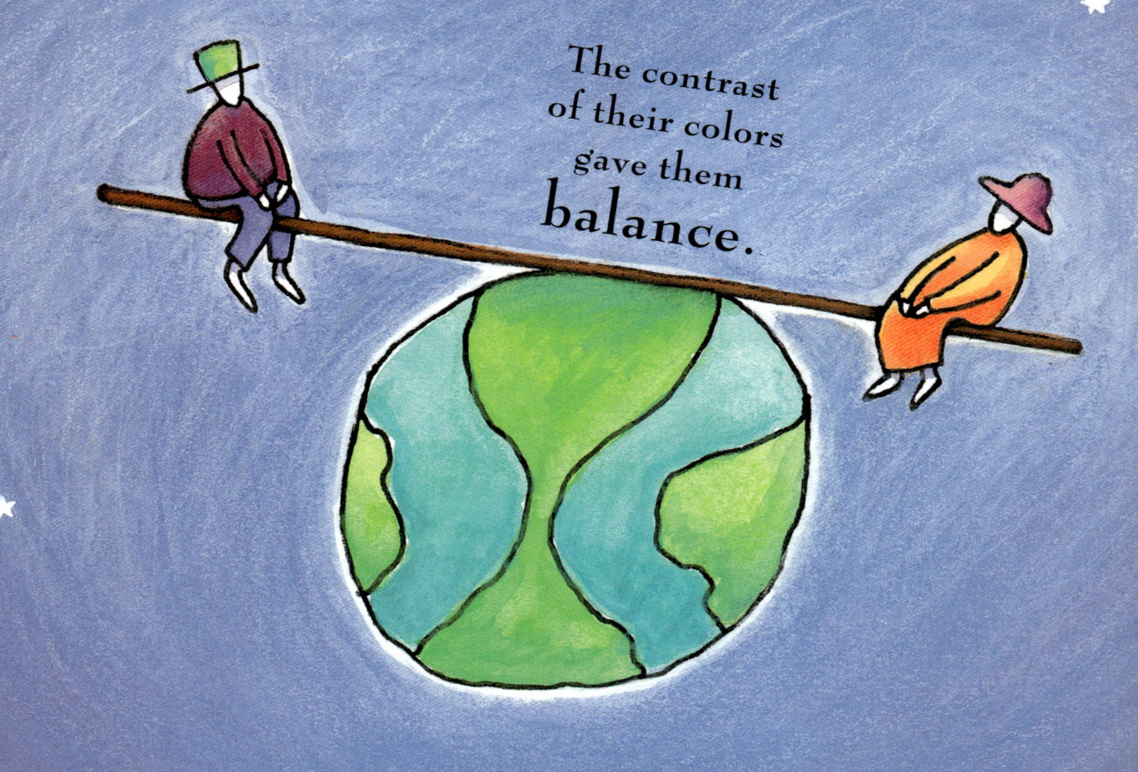

The contrast of their colors gave them **balance.**

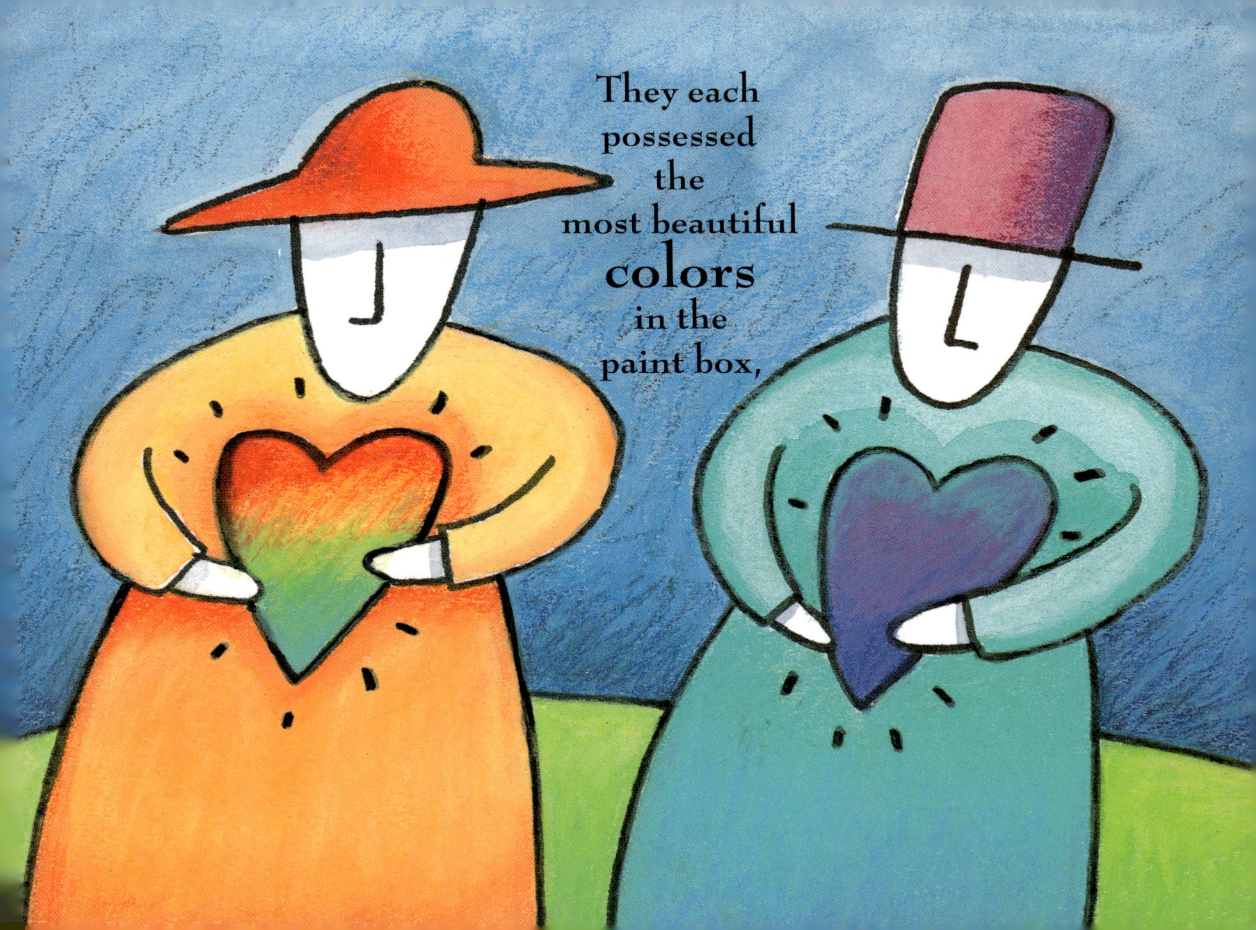
They each
possessed
the
most beautiful
colors
in the
paint box,

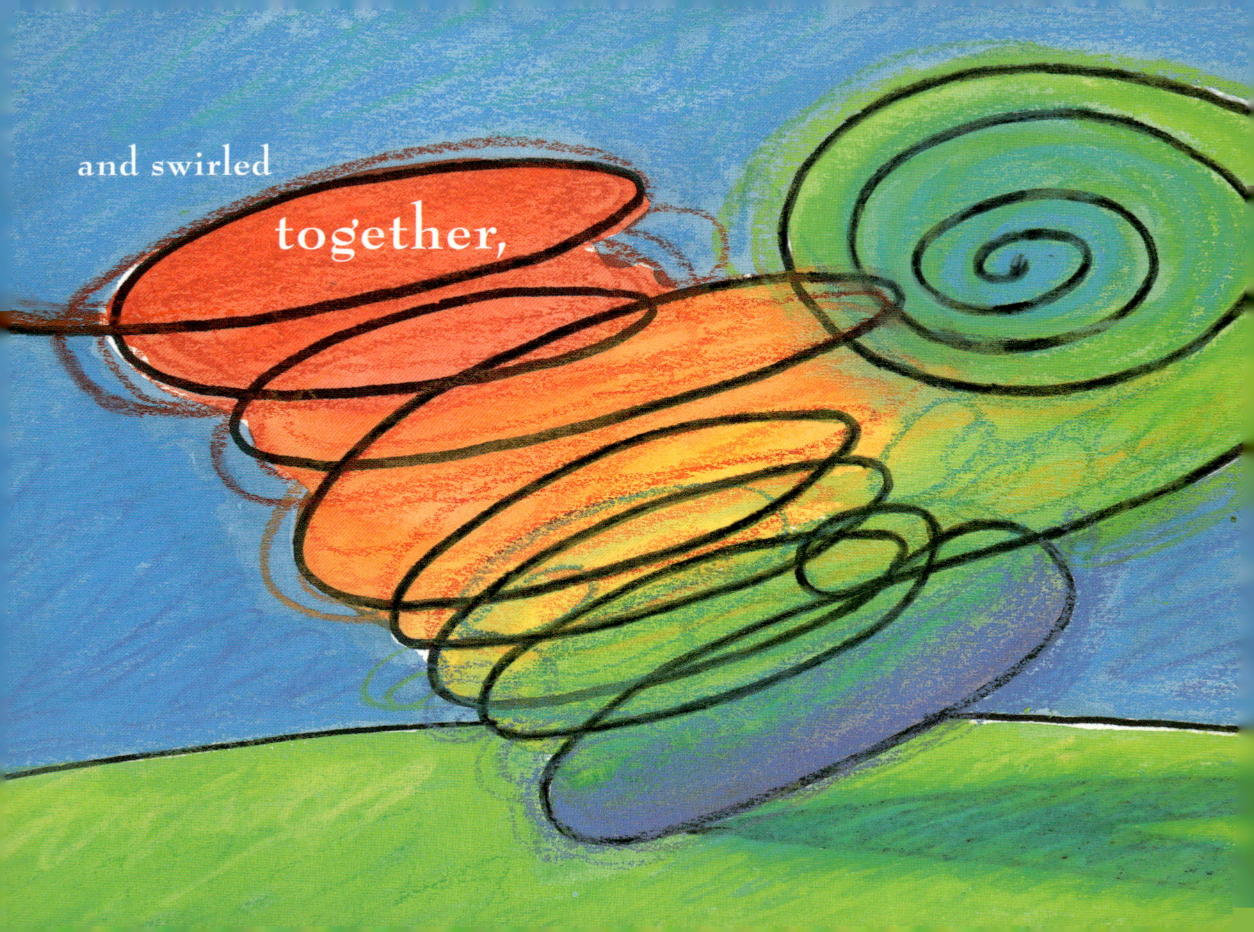

and swirled

together,

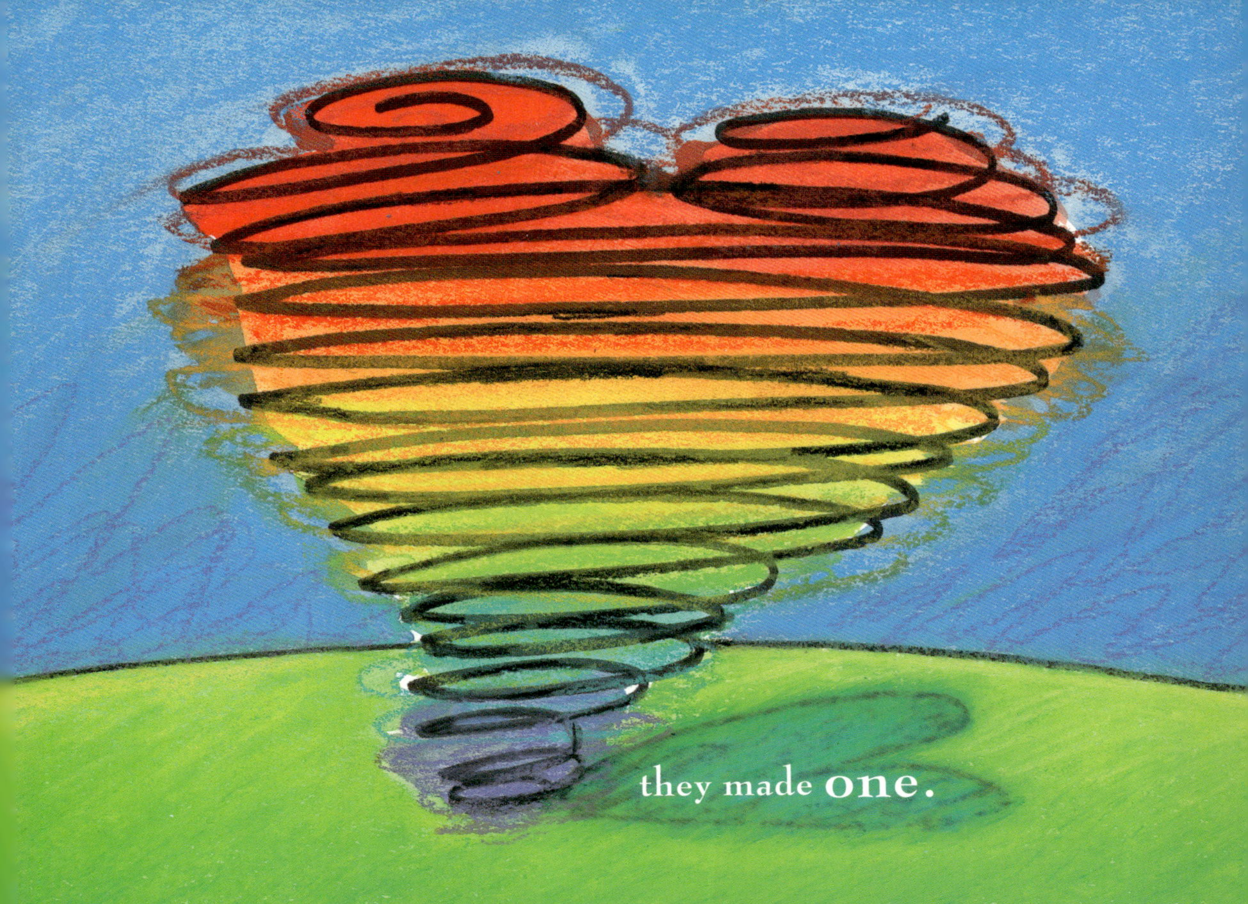
they made one.

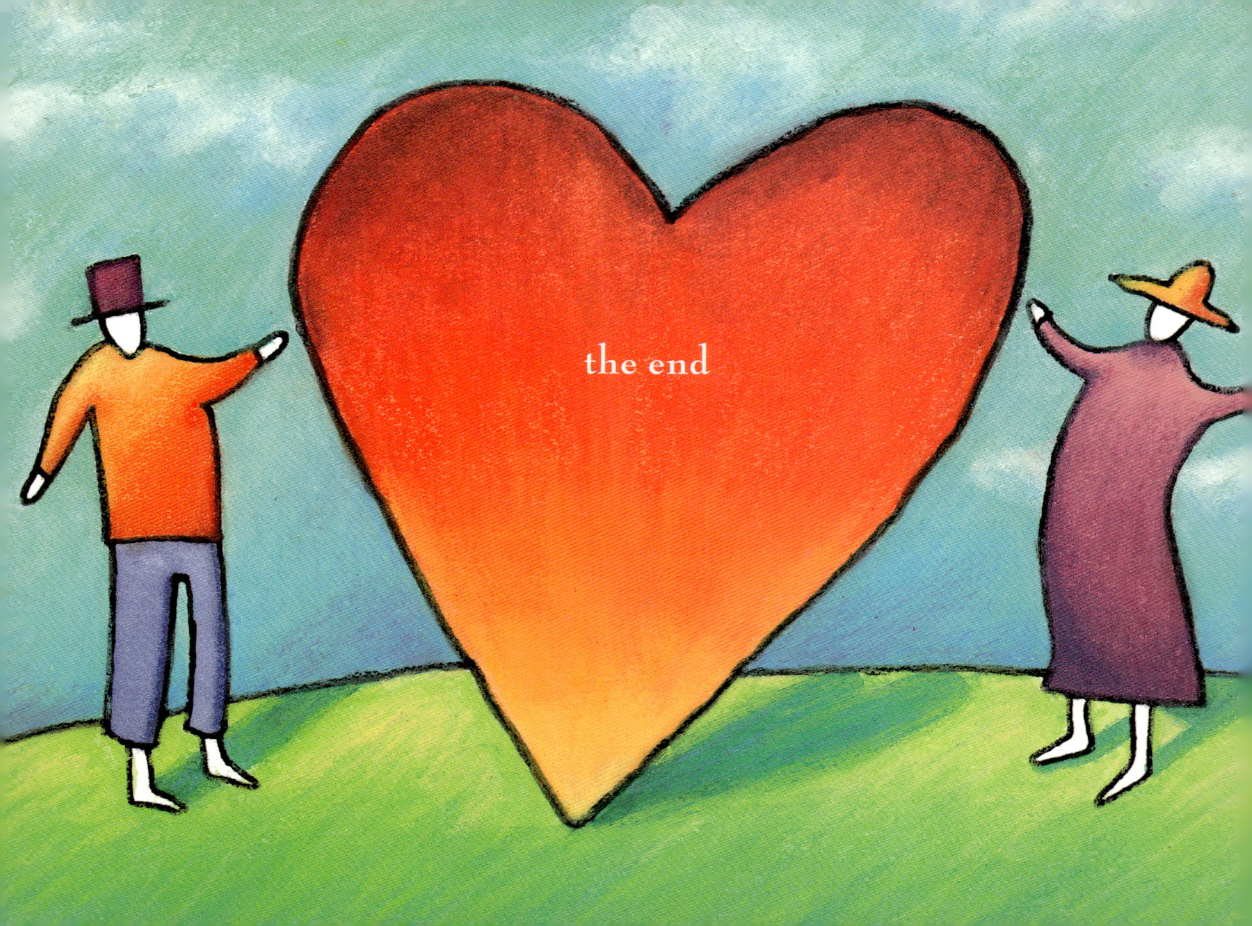
the end

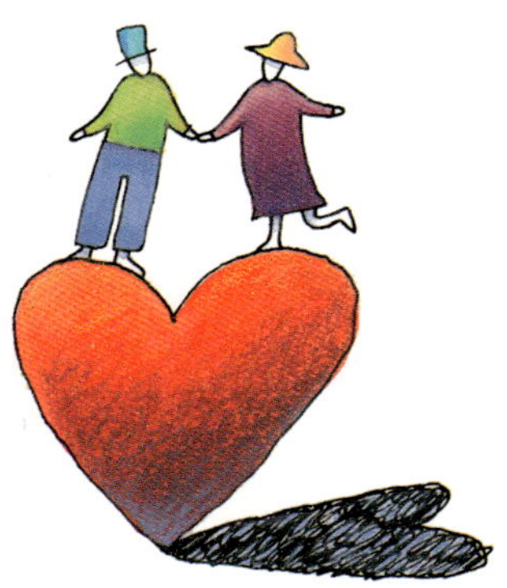

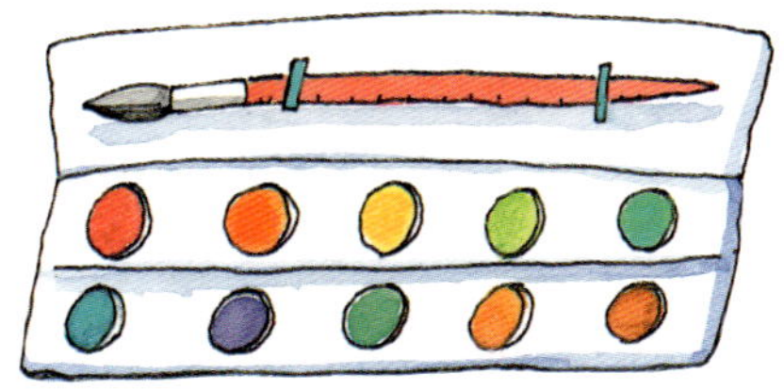